Marilyn's Style

Travilla

This book is dedicated to my Mother,
who has always loved and supported me
unconditionally, even when life got difficult.
*   You are my Mum, my friend, my world.*
Thank you. I love you very much!

THIS IS A GOODMAN BOOK

This edition published in 2017 by
Goodman Books
a division of the Carlton Publishing Group
20 Mortimer Street
London W1T 3JW

A CIP catalogue record for this book is
available from the British Library.

10 9 8 7 6 5 4 3 2 1

ISBN 978 1 84796 097 9

This book was first published in 2011 under
the title *Dressing Marilyn*.

Printed and bound in China.

Marilyn's Style

The Timeless Dresses of William Travilla. Designed for a Hollywood Star

Andrew Hansford

GOODMAN

Contents

A Note from Linda Gray

My dear Andrew,

I wanted to tell you how excited I am to have been asked to write the foreword to your book about Bill Travilla. Sometimes someone comes into your life that will put a smile on your face and leave you with the fondest of memories. Bill Travilla was such a person.

When I was first told that the great Bill Travilla was going to be the next designer for *Dallas*, I immediately flashed back to the iconic white dress that he designed for Marilyn Monroe and couldn't believe that he would be designing for us.

I was immediately enthralled by his design sense, his personality and his humour. He had the most amazing twinkle in his eyes and I felt that we would get along famously. We did!

He loved women and he loved dressing them. I can remember the way the fabrics would feel and the shape that Bill would design to compliment your body. The world was watching and they wanted to see glamour. They did! When you are doing a scene you don't want to be concerned about the fit of your clothes, or fiddling with a skirt or a strap that doesn't fit properly. You simply want to know that the outfit is perfect so that you can focus on your work. Bill made that possible.

I have a few of the sketches that he did for me and they will always remain in my scrapbook of special memories of the *Dallas* years spent with an extraordinary human being whom I loved dearly. His memory will stay with me forever as a talented, creative and charming designer that will always bring a smile to my face. I can see him smiling right now!

Andrew, when we met it was love at first sight and I feel that Bill would have been extremely happy that we did.

With Love

An Interview with the Author

Both Marilyn Monroe and William Travilla made a monumental leap from modest backgrounds to the unreal world of Hollywood stardom and in many ways the story of how Andrew Hansford, the author of this book, was catapulted into this world of glamour, sophistication and drama is just as extraordinary.

Andrew may have been familiar with glamorous lifestyles, having worked in the world of fashion and celebrity as both a model and a hairdresser before setting up his own business in the beauty industry, but the degree to which he was about to be immersed in this lost silver-screen world and the responsibility he would have thrust upon him would overwhelm most people. In the autumn of 2007 a phone call out of the blue from an old and forgotten friend changed everything. As Andrew explains:

"It was early evening in September 2007 and I was talking with a dear friend in the States with whom I'd lost contact many years before. I said I could do with a little PR lift for my business and casually he suggested he send over one of Marilyn Monroe's dresses to put in the window for a little publicity. Of course I laughed it off. Then a week later a courier arrived with not one dress but a huge box of dresses, all by William Travilla and including some of the stunning prototype costumes he had designed for Marilyn Monroe's most famous movie roles."

As Andrew unpacked dress after dress he began to realize the scale of what was being offered to him. "Who would have thought that this man and this random reconnection would turn my world around but it did!"

And he quickly realized that the contents of these boxes were far more than a gift to give a struggling business a PR kick. They were something that would be of huge interest to the wider world too. It was then that he made the decision to mount an exhibition featuring the most well known of the dresses.

Incredibly, just six weeks later "The Lost Dresses of Marilyn Monroe" exhibition was on the eve of opening in the UK, thanks to a whirlwind of help from friends and contacts of Andrew's. "Lighting designers, set dressers – everyone pulled together, desperate to help. But then that's the kind of feeling Marilyn inspires in people."

Perhaps naively, Andrew had anticipated only modest interest, until a PR friend pointed out the magnitude of what was about to appear: "I remember her saying to me 'This is going to be big!'" laughs Andrew as he recollects the conversation. "To me it was just seven dresses in a huge ballroom, pulled together on a shoe-string… it was only when I arrived for the press-call that I realized quite how big it was going to be. There were hundreds of press there and they stayed for hours."

ABOVE Andrew Hansford, the author and the curator of the estate of William Travilla.

And because of the extraordinary and irreplaceable value of the dresses, the exhibition venue refused to allow them to be kept there overnight, leaving Andrew himself responsible for the collection. "Eventually I had to take them out of the back door to stop people following me," he explains, "and there I was taking them back to my own flat – these extraordinary relics of Hollywood history."

Andrew Hansford is frank about his lack of knowledge about the dresses compared with most of the people who came to see the exhibition. He says, "Take 'Sue the Stalker' – a nickname meant in the nicest possible way! – for example. There was this blonde woman sitting in the audience as I introduced the dresses. People were firing questions at me about Marilyn and the dresses and she was sitting there, arms crossed, with a face that said she knew I was out of my depth. Someone asked a question that I just didn't know the answer to but I had a feeling she probably would, so I turned and pointed to her and said 'I don't know but she does!' And I was right, she knew everything there was to know about Marilyn and was happy to have the spotlight turned on her!"

In fact, Andrew quickly realized that listening to Marilyn's fans would give him a fresh insight into the unique appeal of this Hollywood legend. As Sue, who confesses she has read over 100 books on Marilyn, pointed out, "If Andrew was going to deal with the dresses of this famous icon he had better get to know a little more about her!" From her reaction and that of other die-hard fans to the dresses, the magnitude of what he had to offer quickly became apparent. Sue describes seeing the dresses for the first time:

"I found a treasure trove of fabulous items, most of which I recognized from her films. I wandered round to peek behind the gold lamé dress when a man rushed over to ask what I was doing. This was my first meeting with Andrew. We then talked for probably close to an hour, him telling me about Travilla, the designs and history of the dresses, as well as wonderful stories about Marilyn and I, in turn, told Andrew a little of this wonderful lady's life story.

"When I visited the dresses in Bath, Andrew kindly showed me some that were not even on display. I asked if I could touch one and, although he looked at me as if I were some crazy woman, he let me. He will never know how much that meant to me but all the Marilyn Monroe fans out there certainly will.

"Andrew asked me why Marilyn means so much to me. It is because she embodies everything that is womanly – the curves, the laugh and the sexuality she oozes – but also she could be a tough cookie, taking on the studios which was not done at that time. Yet, at the same time, she had this vulnerable side which makes you want to protect her. I also think she was clever. She played the dumb blonde but, if you read any interviews she gave, you will invariably find a sharp and witty comeback to some question or other. Her comic timing is impeccable and I believe that many of the problems you hear about her on set were just her getting her own way with the lines – she steals every scene she is in with ease, even when playing alongside some of the greats.

"I know I am not the only one who is fascinated by this lady and it is wonderful that Andrew is helping her image and personality stay alive through showing these dresses and telling her stories."

Following the exhibition and the revelation of quite how devoted to Marilyn so many people were, Andrew started to see the big the possibilities of touring with Travilla's designs for Marilyn. He soon realized he had to visit the States to learn more.

The many costumes designed by William Travilla and the dresses exhibited by Andrew that first time in Brighton are part of an extensive collection held by Bill Sarris, Travilla's long-time business partner and friend. When Travilla died in 1990 he bequeathed his personal collection to Sarris but, as Andrew explains:

"Bill had done little with the collection, in essence because many people are only interested in Travilla's very famous muse rather than making Travilla the household name he deserves to be. Bill Sarris' wish is that Travilla will become recognized as the tremendous designer that he was, over and above the costumes he created for Marilyn.

"The collection had never left the United States and now is in my keeping in the United Kingdom. I cannot begin to explain the incredible trust and generosity Bill has shown to me. There are very few times in life when you witness such an unselfish act. But Billy Travilla loved the UK and had a huge following here – he spent three months here before going to Paris for the filming of *Gentlemen Marry Brunettes* (1955) with Jane Russell and he had a couture fashion line in this country, so it was an obvious place to start the costume tour."

The magnitude of the archive held by Sarris, not to mention the fact that Sarris himself was a character to be reckoned with, was something that Andrew was unprepared for when he finally visited Sarris in his Palm Springs house.

"The first time I met Bill I feared him, but once you get to know him, he is so funny! I arrived to stay at the house – which in itself was like nothing I had seen before – and for a couple of days I was terribly polite and British and didn't ask to see the dresses or sketches. Then finally Bill just said to me, 'Don't you want to see them then?'

"At first I didn't even realize what was there: a few sketches of Marilyn, Travilla's Oscar… then in the bedroom I opened the closet door and – it sounds like a cliché – I literally fell to my knees. I closed the door and went to the second bedroom, then Bill's bedroom and a three-car garage – all full of boxes. There was a cupboard with sketches, floor to ceiling. It was incredible.

"There was so much that I wheeled a clothes rail out and simply pulled out what I thought was pretty. I was 99 per cent right, even with an untrained eye, because the couture dresses, the costumes and Oscar dresses are so stunning they jump out at you. The quality is unmistakable, with hand-sewn seams and rolled hems. And then there were the sketches… it was ridiculously big, monumental even. There were sketches, patterns and, bit by bit, it became exciting. A pattern for *The Seven Year Itch* (1955) dress, for example – I screamed when I saw that. And there were sketch designs for *Valley of the Dolls* (1967) and Judy Garland – it all came back with me to England."

Why Sarris decided that now was the time to bring this archive to light and that Andrew Hansford was the man to do it becomes clearer when you meet Andrew. His raw enthusiasm, tempered with an acknowledgment of how much he still has to learn and his sheer determination to do right by the memory of William Travilla and by Sarris (who is suffering from Alzheimer's disease; part of the proceeds from the Travilla Tour go to the British Alzheimer's society) combine to make him the perfect choice to show the collection.

For many years Sarris shunned the limelight and refused offers from less than scrupulous people hoping to get their hands on the collection, mostly because of the Marilyn dresses. Andrew is perhaps one of the few who have really taken on board the significance of Travilla's work which goes beyond the costumes he designed for Marilyn. As Andrew points out, "Travilla dressed around 270 stars and designed for more than 100 movies and television series, culminating in him becoming an Oscar-winning designer. He really was a god of the fashion world."

But Andrew admits it is hard work handling a legacy that is linked with one of Hollywood's greatest icons. "People say I have the best job in the world but it's not always like that. It's a privilege, but essentially I'm living vicariously through someone else's talent. I've learned a lot about myself and have developed a tremendous respect for the business of costume design. I might even have become a designer if I had discovered all this earlier," he laughs.

His image of Marilyn Monroe has also changed through meeting people who actually knew the actress so famous for the frothy persona that belied her true self. "Both Travilla and Bill Sarris were very good friends with Marilyn Monroe throughout her life and I have been privileged enough to hear many famous anecdotes from Bill himself, some of which are featured in this book. I now have a great picture of her that is so different from reading books or made-up stories; the real version bears no relation to what the existing books on Marilyn tell us."

At times, you get the feeling that Andrew Hansford can't quite believe what he is doing and on occasion he even ends up in some sitcom-worthy situations. For example, he tells the hilarious story of how Bill Sarris loaned him

ABOVE The fashion designer (most notably of Diana, Princess of Wales's wedding dress) David Emanuel, who opened the exhibition in Bath of Marilyn's dresses.

Travilla's Oscar statuette in order to lend more validity to the clothes on exhibition.

"He said to me, 'Take this… to prove nothing is fake.' So I did, in my hand luggage, back to the UK. Of course, as soon as I went through security my bag was scanned and, before I knew it, all these guards came out of nowhere and pinned me against a wall. I didn't have time to say anything – I couldn't understand why they had attacked me. They kept saying something about a lethal weapon and of course I argued back. I had no idea what they were talking about. Finally, they seized my bag and took out the Oscar, wrapped in a tea towel! I couldn't help but laugh, which probably wasn't the most sensible reaction, but finally I unwrapped it and showed it to the group of security guards.

"What happened next, you've never seen anything like it. They all wanted to touch it, have their photo taken next to it and me. They went from being suspicious of me to treating me like a hero – in fact, I think they thought the Oscar was mine. I even heard someone ask if I was Hugh Grant! After that I was allowed to board my plane but by then word had got around and everyone kept coming up to me and asking, 'Are you the guy with the Oscar?' So I had to keep getting it out. By the time we were airborne it was being handed round the cabin as everyone oohed and aahed over it. Well, it couldn't go anywhere when we were 35,000 feet up in the air, could it?"

Though this attitude to such a precious object might seem flippant, in fact, it shows the refreshingly normal, un-star-struck side to Andrew Hansford. And it is precisely this quality that makes him such a perfect choice to bring these iconic dresses to the public. There is no sycophancy about him in relation to either Marilyn Monroe or to William Travilla. There is a genuine respect for the quality of creation that was achieved within their unique working relationship but, essentially, you get the impression that his priorities are to honour the trust Bill Sarris has shown him – as Andrew puts it, "He is the life-force behind Travilla" – and finally, most importantly, to do justice to the genius and the memory of William Travilla.

Karen Homer

OPPOSITE A publicity shot of Travilla's workroom. The mannequins show the names of Jean Simmons, Joan Collins and Marilyn Monroe.

Introduction

Fifty years on, classic Hollywood films still enthral us. The years have not diminished their power to seduce us into a world where men are men and women are goddesses. Hollywood offered a visual illusion of perfection with stars that looked more desirable, more fashionable and more iconic than in real life. The unsung hero of the film world, responsible for creating these perfect images for so many legendary actors, was the costume designer.

This book is dedicated to one such designer, Mr William "Billy" Travilla. It details the early years of his life, when he could be described as a child prodigy, through his later career where his brilliance as a costume designer and the work he did dressing his muse, Marilyn Monroe, saw him create some of the most iconic dresses of the silver screen.

Loved by many and respected by all, this Oscar-winning designer deserves his place in the Hollywood hall of fame, along with some of his better-known contemporaries, many of whom pursued the limelight, while Travilla avoided it. He possessed the looks of a Hollywood star, the humour of a comedian and the warmth of a true friend and underneath it all were his raw talent and genius for design, complemented by his ability to think creatively and his love and understanding of women.

It was thanks to a chance meeting that his life was turned upside down and he became one of the greats of costume history. That meeting was with the one and only Marilyn Monroe. Throughout his career Travilla designed for eight of her films, dressing her in his signature style of pleating and bias-cut dresses that draped and moulded themselves to the actress in a suggestive yet censor-eluding manner. He also maintained a friendship with Monroe that would endure to the end of her life, always loving and respecting who she really was. He never forgot how hard she worked and the sacrifices she made to become the star the world knew.

In the world of film the relationship between costume designer and star often goes unrecognized and in the case of Marilyn Monroe and William Travilla it was a partnership made in heaven. Travilla created some unforgettable dresses: the white halter-neck dress from *The Seven Year Itch* (1955) and the pink dress worn by Marilyn as she sang the unforgettable "Diamonds Are a Girl's Best Friend" in *Gentlemen Prefer Blondes* (1953), along with many others.

Travilla also dressed the likes of Ann Sheridan, Barbra Streisand, Errol Flynn, Joan Crawford and Jane Russell, among others. He left behind an incredible legacy, not just because of his influence over costume design, but also over fashion. He was a unique and enviable talent.

Four years ago I could never have imagined finding myself part of a silver-screen world of glamour and sophistication but sometimes life surprises you. A chance conversation turned into an international tour of dresses aptly named "The Lost Collection", and I found myself writing this book. I wanted to put the story of this astonishing man across in a way he would have appreciated: full of humour, lacking in pomposity and accessible to all. In the incongruous setting of my spare room in the suburbs, I tried but, I have to say, failed to evoke the feeling of the glory days of Hollywood. Eventually, I took a trip to the land of golden stars and hand prints in cement on the Walk of Fame and one of the most globally recognized signs in the world: Hollywood! In a hotel room overlooking that famous sign, finally I felt inspired. This was the beginning of telling the story of designer William Travilla, an incredible man with a long and illustrious career.

Originally I was rather daunted by the prospect of putting Travilla's life down on paper as he had achieved so much of interest. I faced the problem that either the book would become biblical in length or I would have to leave too much out. So, on reflection, I decided to dedicate this book to his early years. Travilla's life was truly incredible during this period when, by pure chance, he met a woman he came to call his muse and his friend.

This book is the culmination of new interviews with people still alive who knew both Marilyn and Travilla, TV interviews, newspaper articles and Travilla's diaries and tapes. It is a look at how this man created some of the most memorable costumes in movie history. As his fame is inextricably attached to these dresses the chapters tell the story of each one, from his inspiration and his amazing sketches (worthy of being considered art in their own right) to the most complex patterns, through to final completion, plus all the fun and drama that went with it. There are reasons why some of his costumes became so famous, which you will find out later. However, there are many others that are less well known but just as stunning. This book reveals his scope through his designs for Marilyn Monroe.

So let me take you into a world now mostly forgotten; a world of glamour and sophistication. Here the famous had glossy public personas but behind closed doors were something else entirely. This is the story of one man's life and the Hollywood dream!

A testament to William Travilla's early talent comes from Ann Savage. The two first met in in 1943. At that time, Ann was signed to Columbia as an actress, a beginning contract player. Initially, she worked in the "B"-movie unit on serials like *Lone Wolf* and *After Midnight with Boston Blackie* (both in 1943), as well as playing bit parts in musicals, melodramas and Columbia's "A" pictures such as *The More The Merrier* (1943). During this period Travilla also worked on staff for Columbia Pictures as a wardrobe designer. He often designed special gowns for their movies, as well as entire wardrobes for the full cast.

ABOVE Travilla designed costumes for Ann Savage at the start of his career. She would later describe him as "a whole lot of fun" and "a wonderful man!".

Ann Savage and William Travilla met while both were employed on the Columbia Picture film *Two Señoritas from Chicago* (1943). Ann was cast as Maria (one of the señoritas, the other played by New York top model Jinx Falkenburg), along with radio star Joan Davis, a comedienne and eccentric dancer. Interviewed by documentary historian Kent Adamson in 2005, Ann said: "I met Billy in the wardrobe department at Columbia Pictures, he was doing everything on *Two Señoritas*. We hit it off immediately. We really sparked. He had a real sense of humour, and he knew what he was doing.

"Billy and I ended up working together several times at Columbia. I also recommended him for my freelance pictures after Columbia, and bought items for my personal wardrobe from him. Billy was the best designer I ever worked with. He tailored items to fit your body, so that you always looked good from any angle. He never imposed his design on you, he always made the most of what you had to offer.

"Billy was very sensitive to fabric, knew how it would hang on the body and how it would look under the lights on the set. He knew my bones better than I did! He'd say 'Ann, you have lovely long legs, but you have no rear.' My arms were too short for his taste too. He was so funny about it, but he'd make you look and feel like a showgirl. He was the best! His gowns often had gorgeous pleats, which would hang beautifully, and catch light in different ways as you danced. Sometimes he had cutouts to reveal a side or a shoulder or a back. He knew the value of revealing a little flesh. He often used metallics which were still in vogue in those days. He didn't make an entire gown out of silver or gold, but used it in panels, sometimes sections, to capture light. He was a very clever designer, and always made everyone look good. He was wonderful to work with in this regard, he never took risks that might make you look ridiculous, as an Adrian [a prolific costume designer in the 1930s and '40s] might. He was also a lot of fun! A wonderful man!"

On *Two Señoritas from Chicago*, Ann said: "Billy did some nice suits for us, padded shoulders, popular styles for the dialogue scenes. Jinx and I play hotel maids in the movie, and he did clever outfits that had ruffles but were sexy at the

ABOVE Crowds line the street to se the first showing of Jane Russell in *The French Line*. Some church groups banned the movie because of a dance routine featuring a scantilly clad Jane.

OPPOSITE An aerial view of 20th Century Fox studios on the western edge of Beverly Hills, 1940.

same time for our dialogue scenes. Most guys would've pulled them off the rack, but Billy made them special, we looked good as maids, so later when we're starring in a play, it made sense.

"*Klondike Kate* [1943] was set during the gold rush in California in the 1800s. Billy did some striking gowns for me.... so beautiful. This was my first leading role. Even though it was a 'B' picture, Columbia spent a little extra money on it.... [Billy] went out of his way to make my entrance memorable, with a glamorous period outfit, and a large feathered hat. Very striking! What a gentleman! He knew it was an important part for me, and he made me look and feel so beautiful in his clothes. I really loved him for that, so kind. I'll always remember how happy he was for me, and how much extra he put into his work. Wonderful, wonderful man.

"*Ever Since Venus* [1944] was a modern musical, set in the '40s with swing music.... Billy did three looks for me on this one. It was a girl next door ingénue part, so he dressed me in a nice jumper, a little like a bobby sox girl, and then he did a terrific suit, a professional business suit for a woman.... Fit me perfectly. I *loved* wearing his clothes! Then he did a single gown for the end of the movie... something wonderful, and very clever... he was always very smart

LEFT A movie poster in French advertising *The Adventures of Don Juan*, for which Travilla won an Oscar.

ABOVE Elizabeth Taylor at Cinecittà Stuidos filming Cleopatra's spectacular entry into Rome, a scene that required thousands of extras.

about the characters in a movie, and he'd take time to read the script, so he turned this nice, rather sweet girl next door into a swing dance bride-to-be at the end of the picture, through his design. Billy added to the story, by knowing the characters. It was so smart. I never knew another designer who thought the way he did, understood the characters and story and designed, not only for the film, but handled his actors perfectly so they always looked their best!

"I never worked with Billy again after the 1940s. He moved on to 'A' pictures, and became the favourite of many actresses, especially Marilyn Monroe. His work with her, in her early pictures, set her apart from the other starlets. They were perfect for each other. I always understood why she requested him as much as possible, he made everything about her seem exciting and sexy. I stopped making movies and television in the mid '50s. I would run into Billy in town, a party or a reception, and he always treated me wonderfully. Always a kind word and a little kiss. He was always fun and in demand. A guy who was loved by all who knew him. I felt very lucky to know him. It was a privilege to work with him."

To explore the heyday of Travilla's career in Hollywood, what could be a better place to begin than Los Angeles? It can be a cold and intimidating town and when I arrived I felt somewhat lost. Plus, I was filled with dread at the thought of knocking on doors begging for meetings with some of the most important people in the entertainment industry. However, nothing prepared me for what did happen. I can only put it down to the love and respect people still have for Travilla (or maybe it was me being pushy!) but those doors flew open; people could not do enough. 20th Century Fox and Warner Brothers were both extremely welcoming.

I soon learned that, to this day, Travilla has the respect of the industry and I met many people who knew him. His great sense of humour, the twinkle in his eye, his naughty side and, of course, his charm came through every time anyone

LEFT The spectacular chariot race from *Ben-Hur*. This was the largest outdoor set built at the time.

LEFT The spectacular chariot race from *Ben-Hur*. This was the largest outdoor set built at the time.

OPPOSITE TOP Make-up guru Max Factor helps Mary McAllister with her beauty regime.

OPPOSITE MIDDLE American screen siren Rita Hayworth in the 1940s.

OPPOSITE BOTTOM Clara Bow, for whom Max Factor invented the cupid's-bow lip shape.

spoke of him. I can only thank Travilla himself for being as charismatic as he was – it certainly made things easier for me.

Being invited to 20th Century Fox was a real honour as it is a closed lot, unlike many of the other big studios which are open to the public. Once inside, it is the closest you will come to seeing the studios just as they looked back in the glory days. They still have the old sound stages, each identified on the outside by a gold number, within the original gorgeous neo-classical relief. The cafeteria, or commissary as they call it, is still there and quite unchanged, with a wall of Oscars and a sea of tables and chairs once graced by a host of revered stars including Elizabeth Taylor, Marilyn Monroe, Jane Russell, Charlton Heston, Frank Sinatra and Betty Grable. You can almost feel the ghosts of the past all around.

The little bungalows used by the stars are still there. They are all offices now but, apart from a couple with contemporary giveaways like *The Simpsons* posted on the front, they look the same. There is an enormous mural of Marilyn Monroe from *The Seven Year Itch* (1955) on one of the sound stages and below it is the subway entrance and grate used in the movie. As it is a working set, it really is like in the movies, with people running with racks of costumes, golf carts driving in every direction, and turning a corner and being in the middle of a New York street. I found myself smiling constantly and I definitely caught the Hollywood bug; I can only imagine how exciting it must be to work there and be around so much talent.

The costume department was enormous in its day, with a platoon of seamstresses, cutters and pattern-makers as well as contracted costume designers. Each designer had his or her own office where they would spend a lot of time researching the movies they were working on. Beginning with the script, the costume designer, together with the producer, director and sometimes a choreographer, formed an interpretation of the mood and characterization in relation to the film, the artists, sets, make-up and lighting. Costume was considered one of the most important parts of any movie and it had to be just right; budgets were huge and the designers had a tremendous amount of freedom.

When people hear the phrase "film-making", they picture elaborate sets with large complex cameras, lighting and sound booms, but the importance of costumes is often overlooked. Many seem to forget that the right costume can make or break a character. Other than knowing about fabric and cut, costume designers also need to know the characters they are dressing very well. Sometimes they may even have to know more about a particular character than the actor playing the part does. Costume designers also create a personal bond with some of the actors they dress and this was certainly the case with Travilla and Monroe.

Unfortunately the colossal budget-blowing of the 1963 film *Cleopatra*, a major money-loser for the studio, marked the end of the Fox in-house costume department and sadly, owing in part to the chaotic production, a shift away from the traditional studio system in Hollywood. The term "studio system" refers to the practice of large motion-picture studios producing movies primarily on their own lots with actors and all creative personnel under long-term contract. There were eight big players at the time: 20th Century Fox, Metro-Goldwyn-Mayer, Paramount Pictures, RKO Radio Pictures, Warner Brothers, Universal Pictures, Columbia Pictures and United Artists. These studios, the "big eight", ruled that town.

Not only was *Cleopatra* the most expensive film ever made at the time, for many years its star, Elizabeth Taylor, held the world record for the most costumes changes in a single movie; she wore 64 different costumes in that one Egyptian epic. She has since lost the record to Madonna – in the 1996 movie *Evita* the singer-turned-actress managed a staggering 85 costume changes.

After Fox, I was taken on a whistle-stop tour of "the true Hollywood", Culver City. Hundreds of movies have been produced on the lots of its studios (Sony Pictures studios, originally MGM studios, Culver studios and the former Hal Roach studios). These include *The Wizard of Oz*, *The Thin Man* (1934), *Citizen Kane*, (1941), *Rebecca* (1940), the Tarzan series and the original *King Kong* (1933). Marilyn Monroe made three of her early films while under contract to MGM studios in Culver City: *Asphalt Jungle* and *Right Cross* in 1950 and *Home Town Story* in 1951. More recent films made there include *Grease* (1978), *Raging Bull* (1980) and *E.T. the Extra-Terrestrial* (1982). *Gone with the Wind* (1939) was shot there and in fact the house Tara is still there – it was once the offices of David O Selznick, owner of Selznick International Pictures and creator of *Gone with the Wind*. It was amazing to see this very recognizable house in the middle of a busy intersection!

I also saw the Culver Hotel. This pie-slice-shaped hotel has housed many stars as part-time residents, including Clark Gable, Mickey Rooney, Greta Garbo and Judy Garland, plus some more interesting guests including the Munchkins from *The Wizard of Oz*. Reportedly much craziness happened and you can just imagine seeing them all trotting out of the hotel ready for a day's filming!

To me, at Culver City you can feel more movie mania than in Hollywood itself, but then movies weren't made in Hollywood, which was just a housing development named Hollywood Land. So it was nice to see another side of LA and catch glimpses of the past through all the new builds and busy streets like Venice Boulevard. Now a thriving street, it was once the scene of the chariot race in *Ben-Hur* (1959) and was used in parts of *Cleopatra*.

Another building that filled me with interest was the Max Factor Building. This is situated on Hollywood and Highland, just yards from Grauman's Chinese

Gants, Création "GANT PERRIN" PARIS

Sur toutes les lèvres de Paris !

ROUGE MODE   ROSE MODE

Deux nouvelles teintes de rouge "haute-couture"

ROUGE MODE
Jeune, Vivant
et vraiment ROUGE

hi-fi
rouge à lèvres

ROSE MODE
Gai, Etincelant
et vraiment ROSE

MAX FACTOR
HOLLYWOOD

En un seul rouge à lèvres, tout ce que vous pouvez désirer ! ...teintes "haute fidélité", une stabilité et une finesse encore jamais atteintes...
et puis, il est si doux et si lisse sur vos lèvres !..

Theatre where the famous hand prints are. I believe what went on in this building makes it another unsung hero of Hollywood as Max Factor was responsible for the creation of the faces of the most recognizable stars. None of these stars was born looking the way the world came to see them; the raw materials may have been there, but they all needed help, and that help came in the form of Max Factor. I am lucky enough to know Steve and Dee Dee, the new owners and managers of the Hollywood History Museum, housed in the Max Factor Building and dedicated to the world of Hollywood.

As well as housing Max Factor memorabilia, it holds over 10,000 pieces of film treasures, including gowns worn by Marilyn Monroe and Elizabeth Taylor, Cary Grant's Rolls Royce and one of the several pairs of the ruby slippers made for *The Wizard of Oz*. When Max Factor took it over in the 1920s he wanted a building that reflected the glamour of the cosmetics business in Hollywood. The result was a combination of Empire and Art Deco. You enter through dark marble archways into the small museum, which is divided into several rooms. They contain hundreds of autographed photographs of famous stars (who were also studio clients) and Max Factor magazine advertisements featuring Hollywood's leading ladies alongside dresses, wigs, magazine covers, a gleaming Oscar (which Max himself received in 1929 for his unique make-up) and glass cases displaying old-fashioned versions of Max Factor powders, perfumes, lipsticks and other products.

A pioneer in the field of movie make-up, Max Factor invented the first make-up used in a motion picture (a greasepaint in a tube), and went on to become the inventor of lip gloss, pancake make-up and false eyelashes. In fact, not only did Max Factor pioneer screen make-up, he, with his son Frank Factor (who became

ABOVE Marilyn poses for a portrait in 1947, before her transformation to blonde.

OPPOSITE A poster advertising Max Factor make-up, 1958. The text reads "On all the lips of Paris".

known as Max Factor Jnr), popularized the term "make-up" rather than using the more accepted "cosmetics".

The make-up was made on the top floors of the building and there was a glamorous marble-floored salon on the ground floor. Also upstairs was a garage, reachable by the largest elevator in Hollywood, where stars used to store their Packards, Rolls-Royces and Duesenbergs while away on locations. Downstairs there was a bowling alley and nightclub.

The showpiece of the museum for me was the restored Max Factor colour make-up rooms. The "colour harmony" concept developed by Factor was used to find exactly the right colour for his clients. There is a room painted a special green for redheads – in it Lucille Ball got her famous colour, as did Rita Hayworth. A two-tone blue room was where stars like Jean Harlow became blondes. There was a peach and beige room for what Max Factor dubbed "brownettes", such as Judy Garland, and a dusty-pink room for true brunettes. Clients included Joan Crawford and Bette Davis. Distinctive lipstick styles, such as bee-stung lips, vampire lips, rosebud lips and cupid's bow (for Clara Bow) were all invented in these rooms. There are also two strange Max Factor inventions that I loved on display at the museum: the "Beauty Calibrator" is a weird gizmo from 1932 for measuring the face – it looks more like some medieval torture device! And the "Kissing Machine", from 1939, presses two sets of rubber lips together, under 4.5 kg (10 lbs) of pressure, in order to test the indelibility of lipstick.

Early photos of Marilyn show her hair to be a medium brown colour. Throughout the early to mid 1940s Marilyn experimented with various "brownette" to dark blonde shades. But in 1950 Max Factor hit upon the stunning platinum-blonde hair colour that became synonymous with Marilyn Monroe. He realized that the tone of Marilyn's complexion belied the fact that her new hair colour was the colour she was born with. To make matters worse, the camera with its three-strip Technicolor film was not forgiving; its lens magnified everything. So in the blue-hazed room, "For Blondes Only", Max Factor created Marilyn's new complexion which made her look like a natural platinum blonde. The principle of "colour harmony" was simple – if your skin colour looked good in this cool blue colour room, you'd look like a natural blonde on the stage at the movie studio. A testament to how important make-up was to the image of Marilyn Monroe is the fact that in 1999 Christies auctioned one of Marilyn's early make-up kits for $266,500.

It is impossible to write this introduction without mentioning Bill Sarris, the reason for the Travilla Tour and also for this book; truly his generosity knows no bounds. This legendary man is the surviving business partner of William Travilla and the man who independently ran the business side of the fashion label, The House of Travilla, allowing Travilla freedom to design. Bill Sarris is, sadly, suffering from Alzheimer's disease, which is partly what spurred the project on in the first place. But, even though his illness is progressing, Bill still remembers a tremendous amount from the past.

The pair met when Bill Sarris, a young Greek fresh off the family farm in Utah, was studying design at the prestigious Woodbury University in Los Angeles. According to fellow student Michael Novarese, "he was incredibly talented and it came easy to him." At the end of his degree Bill and his fellow students had to create a design for the end-of-term show. Bill turned in the winning design, voted

LEFT Bill Sarris and William Travilla in the early years of their friendship.

for by Travilla himself, who said, "I saw such a natural-born talent in him". The two became instant friends. Just a few years later, in 1952, they opened what would become one of the longest-running couture houses in fashion history, occupying a section of South Grand Avenue in Los Angeles. Bill Sarris and William Travilla were honoured in 2004 with the Woodbury Design Award.

But, however much fun their years together were, there were times when Sarris would lose patience with Travilla. Travilla hated publicity but Sarris knew the importance of PR. Since the 1930s, costume design had hit an all-time high and dressing female stars became a creative effort surpassing even the couture houses of Paris. Costume designers had the power to transform actresses into icons, turning them into the illusions of perfection that put these women in the annals of history and are part of what still attracts us to Hollywood movies today. Yet when Travilla was recognized by a member of the public and stopped in the street or a restaurant, he would always say, "Oh, I'm not Travilla. I just look like him". It frustrated Sarris immensely, although he laughs about it now.

In fact, Travilla never once put himself up for an award (customary practice within the film industry), did not lobby for votes nor asked to be nominated. Nevertheless he was regularly nominated for awards by his peers, who felt he truly deserved the acknowledgement.

Bill Sarris was also a talented designer himself, but he will never admit it and always gives all credit to Travilla. I talked to a few people who had worked with Bill and they said that after they had completed their mock-ups of dresses for an upcoming collection they would call Bill in to look them over. Always polite, he would walk the room and say, "That's lovely, but how about lowering the neck line of that one, shorten that a little, add a jacket…" And he was always right!

Even now, I love to hear his opinions on fashion. He cannot watch the Oscars as he says, "Most of them look awful. Back in my day the stars would come to designers and ask to borrow clothes and if that particular star did not suit the sort of clothing they produced the designer would say 'No'. Nowadays it is the designers who are touting their wares to the stars. An actress could end up with many dresses to choose from. In the past even I have been asked on occasion if a certain celebrity could borrow something from the collection, but hearing their 'stylist' say: 'It has to be a gift, you won't get it back,' well, my answer was

always, 'No way' (or words to that effect). Actually you cannot really call them stars nowadays as there are very few left; it's really all about celebrity."

In Sarris' house are many awards, including some bearing the name of Charles LeMaire, who was the head of costume at 20th Century Fox. Bill, ever loyal, explains: "Even when LeMarie didn't design the costumes himself he got credit, since he was the head of the department. Everyone in the industry knew it was Bill Travilla who did most of the design work there."

As Sarris was around for most of Travilla's career he remembers many wonderful stories. He tells, for instance, how when the pair went to the set together, Travilla would always leave him in the car, promising, "I'll be right back". According to Bill, on many occasions Travilla would be working with Marilyn Monroe and she would come running out of the costume offices saying, "Billy, why did you leave Bill in the car? Come in, Bill, it's boiling out here." Bill remembers: "She was so precious; she was the nicest person ever."

During this period Bill and Marilyn spent time together quite frequently. Marilyn, having found out that Bill was quite partial to prawn cocktail, surprised him with the dish on many occasions. As she always thought of others first, he didn't tell her that frozen prawns and bottled sauce wasn't really his thing! Marilyn also made great scrambled eggs on toast. Bill and Marilyn became firm friends but he also remembers how there were two sides to her – the private side and the Marilyn turned on for the public. He explains that "On many occasions I would be having lunch with her in Hollywood somewhere and one time I said to her, 'Why is it that I am having lunch with one of the most famous women ever and no one recognizes you?' She replied, 'That's because you're having lunch with me and not what people see me as, but watch this!'" And Bill watched as she turned it on, full-on Marilyn Monroe, and the whole room turned and gasped. He remembers giggling at this, thinking how clever she was.

Bill acknowledged that Marilyn "could be difficult with the brass, but she was wonderful with little people like me". He admitted that Travilla and Marilyn had a love affair; as far as he was concerned, Marilyn was in love with Travilla. However, Travilla was married and would not leave his wife. Shortly after this Marilyn married Joe DiMaggio, a marriage that famously ended badly.

Bill shared with me many stories from those days, often at the expense of officialdom or the press. One day the fabulous Ann Sheridan, whom he adored, decided to tease the press by saying she was engaged to a lovely Greek boy called Bill Sarris. The first Bill heard of it was when he was accosted by the press. He immediately called Ann, who found it very amusing. "That'll teach them," she said.

Not all the stories were funny. An anecdote about the actress and singer Dorothy Dandridge offers a poignant reflection on the prejudices of the time. Bill and Travilla had gone to Las Vegas to see her nightclub act, as Travilla had been designing show gowns for her for a while. After the show Travilla asked her to join them for a drink at the bar but she replied, "You know they won't let us black girls in the lounge." So, instead, she asked them up to her room and they had a drink there. "She was truly a lovely lady," remembers Bill.

Despite his illness, during my recent conversations with Bill, he became incredibly animated when talking about the past. In his house is a huge photo album with signed pictures from some of the most famous stars. I gave it to Bill on one occasion and he went through them, telling some very funny stories; watching him talk he became more youthful – it was as if the old Bill came back, if only for a short time. When I looked at him I didn't see a man with a dreadfully cruel illness but a man who had the most incredible life, both through the people he met and the incredible success he achieved. The saddest part is that his life history is fading away and eventually those memories will be lost to him forever. I am glad I have had the chance to talk with him now and make sure his life is recorded.

When I visited him I also wanted to read the biography of Travilla that I had written for this book to Bill, as I needed to make sure it was done in a way that both he and Travilla would have wanted. To say we both got very teary is an understatement. I realized then how vitally important this project is to me and how privileged I am to be doing it.

Bill Sarris has maintained Travilla's legacy since his death. His only wish is to show the world Travilla's incredible talent and much of his enviable archive has been kept under lock and key until now. He is a man of true spirit and kindness, who a couple of years ago said something to me that I have lived by throughout this whole project: "Whether it be my last breath or my last memory, I want you to make Travilla the household name he deserves to be." He also wrote on the front cover of the visitor's book used for the exhibition that has travelled the world the words: "Bill Sarris and William Travilla, one in heaven and one still here."

Thank you, Bill, for your incredible trust in me. I will continue to champion Travilla's legacy and yours to the best of my ability.

ABOVE Bill Sarris and Andrew Hansford celebrate New Year's Eve in 2010.

Travilla: A Biography

W illiam Travilla might not be the household name that Marilyn Monroe has become, but without the vision of this brilliant Hollywood costume designer some of the most iconic images of the Hollywood actress would never have existed. During their intense working relationship Travilla created many of Monroe's most famous costumes, and the outfits he created for her to wear in the films *How to Marry a Millionaire* (1953) and *Bus Stop* (1956) earned him two Academy Award nominations. Their relationship was far more, though: it was a love story between two people who admired and loved each other unconditionally. He said in an interview, "My clothes for Marilyn were an act of love, I adored her." It showed.

Travilla never got caught up in the studio system. He hated publicity and could not stand to be noticed. He said on more than one occasion, "I am a designer, not a celebrity," and resolutely dedicated his life to art and culture. Perhaps it is in part owing to his humility that Travilla's work, despite his famous muse, has been largely forgotten and the man who created some of the most recognizable dresses in history is still a virtual unknown.

However, he left an amazing legacy of work, all unique, that continues to this day to inspire fashion and film designers, as well as a host of celebrities who have worn copies of Travilla's most legendary designs. Unlike nowadays, when there is a huge back catalogue of fashion designs to look back on for ideas, in

LEFT Travilla at his design desk in the Fox studios. On the back wall are three lost sketches of Joan Crawford.

OPPOSITE Travilla with his wife Dona and daughter Nia. The sketches seen in the photo are still part of the estate today.

32

1950s Hollywood Travilla and others like him did not have the option of borrowing from the past; inspiration for a costume drama might come from the 1700s or 1800s but for a fashionable movie they had to rely on their own talent and forward thinking. Luckily Travilla had plenty of natural talent and vision that left his contemporaries trailing in his wake.

It is difficult to overstate the early fashion influence of Hollywood. In 1930 an average of 80 million people attended the movies every week in the United States. The record 4 billion annual moviegoers in 1946 dwarfs the modern high of 1.5 billion. This huge audience for film fashion caused even the Paris-oriented *Vogue* magazine to state in 1938 that Hollywood was "certainly the most perfect visual medium of fashion propaganda that ever existed".

Costume is the second skin of the actor. However, in trying to create this skin conflicts can arise, be they from the demands of the studio, the ideas of producer and director, tight budgets or the likes and dislikes of strong-willed actors. In the old studio system the actors were each developed and groomed with a defined public image. The studios holding their contracts determined those images and costume designers were expected to play a major part in creating and maintaining them. The big stars each played dual roles: as the movie star they had become and the one the audience flocked to see. The drawing power of the individual star was paramount. Studios considered stars investments and the biggest received the attention of top studio designers, expert fitters, seamstresses, embroiderers, hair stylists, make-up artists and various coaches. Actresses had their favourite designers – those they got along with and who made them look memorable – and Travilla was always in demand.

On occasions it was not just Travilla's sartorial expertise that attracted the stars. One of his all-time favourite pin-ups was Mae West and, when he was given the opportunity to meet her and discuss possibly designing some costumes for her, the actress received him wearing 25-cm (10-inch) wedge heels, 5-cm (2-inch) eyelashes and a floor-length negligée. According to Travilla, with a translucent swirl of red satin and chiffon straight off a movie set, she sauntered across the room, sat down beside him and, with a tantalizing wink, took his hand and gently guided it towards her bare breast. Sadly for Ms West, Travilla's reaction did little to inspire her confidence in his talents as a designer and he was shown the door within ten minutes. Given that Travilla was in his very early twenties at the time, this must have been an incredibly intimidating experience!

ABOVE LEFT Travilla's first girlfriend, a famous headliner at the Burlesque clubs. She was 15 years his senior and her name was Rose La Rose. The inscription reads:
To Bill
A great artist
Lots of luck and happiness always
Rose La Rose
xx

ABOVE CENTRE An autographed picture given to Travilla of the stunningly beautiful Hedy Lamarr. . She vary rarely gave autographs.

ABOVE RIGHT Travilla's friend and the woman that was to change the course of his life forever, Auntie Ann – Ann Sheridan. The now-faded writing reads::
Dear Billy T
Here's to your lovely designs for all the glamorous bitches you can get your measuring tape around.
Love
Ann

OPPOSITE A sketch from 1934 by Travilla, aged 16. It is a homage to the burlesque clubs he frequented.

Travilla was not the first great costume designer. Adrian, for example, was an MGM studio designer who reached the height of his career in the 1930s and '40s with creations for, among other movies, *The Wizard of Oz* (1939). But if Adrian is credited with bringing glamour to the silver screen, then Travilla must be given credit for injecting sex appeal, and not only because of Marilyn Monroe.

Born on Catalina Island, just off the California coast, in March 1920, William Travilla seemed destined to have some kind of career in the entertainment industry. His father and two uncles travelled the vaudeville circuit as "The Three Travillas", demonstrating their aquatic abilities in onstage performances with the assistance of Trixie the trained seal. And his aunt, under the name Sylvia Travilla or Seelie, was a silent-screen actress who was one of two favourite leading ladies of Buster Keaton.

Travilla himself showed a passion for art from a very young age. He attended the prestigious Chouinard School of Art in Los Angeles, where he advanced to adult classes at the age of just eight. By the time he reached his mid teens the burlesque clubs that he passed on his way to school began to pique his interest and he started frequenting them. Here he moved his artistic talent on to a commercial level by selling costume sketches to the dancers for around $5.

At an early age he inherited $5,000 from his grandfather and decided to experience the world. He and a cousin spent almost a year travelling through the South Seas, and during his time in Tahiti Travilla was inspired to paint a stunning set of portraits of the islanders. On arriving back in the United States he landed his first film job, at the legendary Western Costume Company, where he began ghost-sketching costume drawings for studio designers. This proved to be an invaluable learning experience, giving Travilla an insight into the business of costume design. After Western he took a job at another busy Hollywood costume shop, Jack's of Hollywood. It was here that he acquired his first big-name client, Sonja Henje, as well as working on assignments for United Artists and Columbia.

Despite working in the costume business, at this point in his life Travilla was still captivated by his time in Tahiti and, in great need of earning some money, he produced a series of paintings of semi-nude Tahitian beauties on black velvet. These pictures were to change the course of his life. Exhibiting them at a famous local hot spot called Don The Beachcomber, a tropically decorated bar popular with Hollywood celebrities, Travilla was discovered by a young woman who began collecting his work. This was the actress Ann Sheridan, later referred to by Travilla as "Auntie"; they built up a friendship, and she eventually brought him to the Warner lot to become her personal costume designer, earning the significant sum of $400 a week. Travilla went on to create dresses for Sheridan for her films *Nora Prentiss* (1947) and the period drama *Silver River* (1948).

In August 1944 Travilla married the stunning starlet Dona Drake. Drake was already a huge success on the Hollywood scene so it was a perfect match. The pair were madly in love and, despite the objections of everyone they knew, within ten days of meeting they were man and wife. Travilla and Dona certainly made a fascinating combination. Both were very attractive. Dona, being six years older than Travilla, was more guarded and wiser in the ways of the world. She too was a child prodigy, who by the time she reached the age of 13 was on the road with a girl band. At 16 she became the girlfriend of a notorious gangster who was gunned down only months after they met, and when she was 17, the studios

OPPOSITE Travilla's Certificate of Nomination from the Academy. He won the Oscar for Best Color Costume Design for his outfits for *The Adventures of Don Juan*.

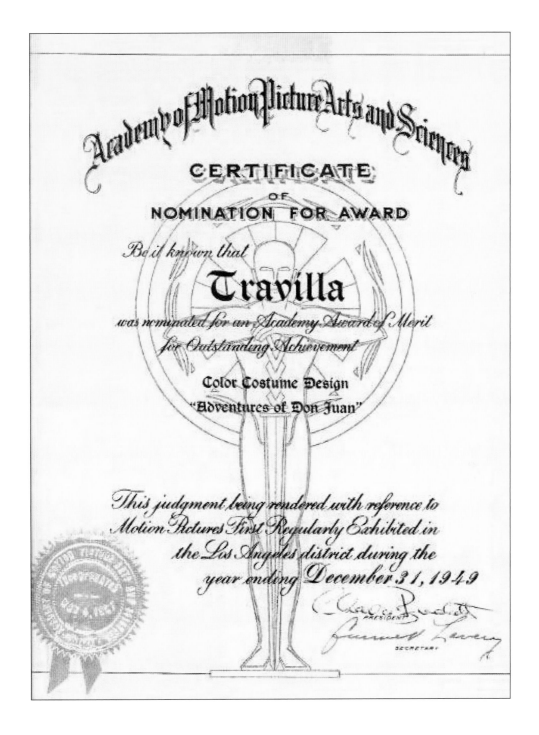

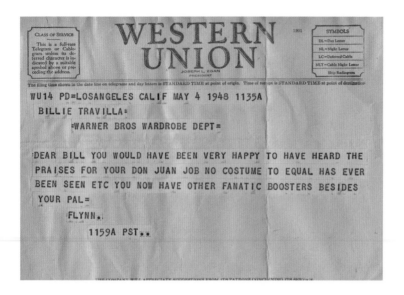

discovered her singing in a nightclub and put her under contract. As was the custom of the day, they changed her name and gave her a new past; during the course of her career she was to appear in 25 films. Exotically beautiful, Dona was the pin-up girl of choice at the time she met Travilla. The couple had one child together, a daughter named Nia, who was born in 1951.

Ann Savage recalls, "Dona Drake was a firecracker, and hated to let him out of her sight. She went everywhere with a trained leopard, a very exotic Spanish lady, with a quick temper! She was out on tour frequently, and when she'd come back, she'd raise hell with everyone around Billy. She knew he was a character, and everybody loved him, so she'd try to find out what kind of trouble he was up to while she was gone! They were a fun couple, beautiful together… always got a kick out of them!"

They both had a taste for the exotic too. At one time in their house lived an ocelot (called Errol after Errol Flynn), two huge scarlet and blue macaws, a pair of giant white cockatoos, a banana-billed toucan, tanks filled with multi-coloured fish and, the *pièce de résistance*, a woolly monkey called Johnny.

However, Dona Drake's past would have made a movie in itself. There was more to her than Travilla or anyone else realized. Dona had been keeping a secret since childhood, the kind of secret that left her on guard every minute of every day and one that, should it have been revealed, could have torn her life apart. To put her story in context, in 1949 director Elia Kazan made the film *Pinky*, starring Jeanne Craine. Craine was considered extremely daring to have taken the risk of portraying the central character of the film, that of a light-skinned child of black parents who runs away to a strange city and lives the ultimate lie: passing as a white girl. There were some people who predicted that Craine would throw away her career, leaving it irreparably tarnished by taking on this role. But, despite these facts, the film was a landmark movie of its time, radically explosive and aimed straight at the heart of spoken and unspoken racial hatred within the fabric of the culture.

ABOVE LEFT A personal telegram from Errol Flynn congratulating Travilla on winning his Oscar.

What was not known to Travilla or anyone else was that Dona Drake was the living embodiment of this shocking movie. It was a secret that she kept even from her husband for many years and one that he went to his grave without revealing. Interracial marriage was not only frowned upon but illegal in most of the United States at the time, and even "liberal" Hollywood could not escape bigotry and ignorance. Bill Sarris has asked for the story of Dona's life to be told now to illustrate the sickening oppression of this era.

It was at Warner Bros that Travilla successfully broke into the hierarchical world of costume design when he was asked by the legendary actor Errol Flynn, who had admired his work with Sheridan, to design costumes for his role in the 1948 movie *The Adventures of Don Juan*. The original stock of costumes by Edith Head was tossed out because they were considered too flouncy and Errol hated them, and Travilla was rushed in to replace her. Errol commented that, "if he can make that old war horse Sheridan look good, he can do it for Uncle Errol."

It was not easy working with the likes of Flynn. He and Travilla argued at length over every seam in his costume and Errol spent hours over the simple fitting of a collar, saying again and again to Travilla, "Oh no, we were better off the way we had it before, Bill." This constant interference had Travilla climbing the walls with frustration but the resulting huge expenditure and time taken to create the perfect costume did not bother Errol at all. His ego – and, as was often the case, a little too much alcohol – fortified him against criticism. But Flynn, the major star, liked Travilla, the young designer, from the moment he met him. Flynn called Travilla "Little B" or "Little Bill" and told Travilla to call him "Uncle Errol".

During the filming of *The Adventures of Don Juan* Travilla was called at home by the director, who said that Errol was furious, complaining that his costumes did not work, and Travilla had better go to the set as filming was being held up. Travilla, in blind panic and in fear of losing his job, rushed to Errol's dressing room, where he found Errol seated at the make-up table with his tights rolled down past his knees, holding a fake vibrator. "How do I get this into my pants?" he asked, laughing uncontrollably. Travilla, whose first reaction was one of shock and relief that his job was safe, then started to laugh along with Errol.

Travilla wasn't the only one to suffer. Errol's humour and practical jokes were legendary and tested the patience of everyone on set, including the Swedish newcomer Viceca Lindfors. In one scene, Errol, wearing tights and boots, was stripped bare to the waist and facing the mirror, shaving, when the actress entered and began to deliver her lines, word perfect as usual. As he turned to her, she glanced down to discover that, instead of the regular double pair of tights, Errol was wearing a sheer single pair and was enormously glad to see her. She turned beet-red, stumbled back and completely blew her lines. Needless to say, Errol Flynn was laughing hysterically.

Some people commented that the *Don Juan* costumes were not totally true to the period. As Travilla said, "my research showed that men in that period were all bloomers, ruffles and face powder, but Errol took one look and said, "'Not for old Dad!'" So Travilla created his very own period look, putting Flynn in doublets with plunging necklines and tights, certainly a very sexy take on the traditional costumes of the period. Travilla's stamp has been on every pirate and swashbuckler film from that day forward.

ABOVE Travilla and his wife Dona, seen here cutting out the fabric for a swimming costume.

In the end, Travilla and Errol got on famously and both the movie and costumes for *The Adventures of Don Juan* were a great success. Incredibly, so early in his career, with this first independent foray into costume design Travilla was nominated for, and went on to win, an Academy Award. The studio outdid itself for the premiere, sending a champagne and pearl-white limousine to pick up Travilla and Dona. Travilla had designed an extraordinary gown for his wife and they dominated the red carpet that night. Unsurprisingly, he was soon offered a contract with 20th Century Fox, where he encountered a certain blonde.

William Travilla first met Marilyn Monroe in 1950 when working on a film with Gene Tierney. Monroe had done *Asphalt Jungle* (1950) and played other small parts but she was not yet the big star that she was destined to become. But the actress was very aware of how to promote herself, knew that publicity was the only way she would be seen by millions and was determined to get her picture taken at every opportunity. She realized early on that it was important to let the world know she was there, even when the studio wasn't doing much with her. Marilyn once told Travilla how she had adored Jean Harlow and Clark Gable as a kid, collecting all their photos. He later said, "I know one thing, she became bigger than Jean Harlow and her last movie had Clark Gable as her leading man, so she did get what she wanted, she did bigger and better."

Her willingness to pose for photographs set her apart from some of her more reluctant contemporaries and she was loved by the photographic gallery at the film studio for it. While other young actresses were too busy doing other things to worry about publicity, Marilyn would come in at any time, often borrowing clothes from the wardrobe department. Travilla's office was along one side of the wardrobe building and, as a contracted designer, he was always there.

One day Marilyn popped into the offices and, always formal at the start of their relationship, said, "Mr Travilla, I need to try a few things for these publicity photos, would it be possible to use your fitting room?" Travilla was more than willing to comply. He had a very long and narrow room, divided by sliding doors; one side was his office where he would work on his drawings or research scripts, the other comprised a dressing area with a three-way mirror on a desk. Marilyn went and changed into the things she had brought with her. Then she popped her head out and asked, "Do you like this?" As she stepped out of the fitting room the strap on the bikini she was wearing broke and her left breast fell out.

This was Travilla's first introduction to Marilyn Monroe. At this time, although she made friends with the photographers and wardrobe departments, the bigger fish was Travilla, and Marilyn knew this. On many occasions after that she would come to his offices and try things on. Once she brought some things in to get his opinion. Travilla wasn't too happy with her choices so went into the costume stock to find her something else and grabbed a few things he thought would work better and look great in photographs. He was right, so, little by little, Marilyn started to come to him for help. She trusted him totally and continued to do so with everything he ever made her, and their relationship became increasingly intimate.

Around their second or third meeting Travilla had collected a big box of fox furs from a period film he was working on. He told Marilyn to take all her clothes off and just wrap herself in them. So she did, unhesitatingly stripping

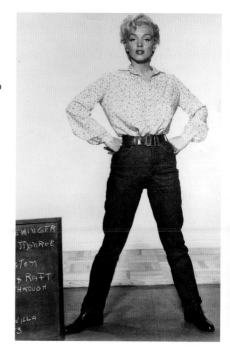

ABOVE Costume test shot of Marilyn Monroe for *River of No Return*.

RIGHT Marilyn Monroe and Harry Weston in a publicity shot for *River of No Return* (1945). These two images show the very different styles of costume Travilla had to create for Marilyn for this movie.

> ## *She was the most complex, incredible, magnificent woman. She was the love of my life that girl.*

Travilla on Marilyn

nude, and when she opened the doors of the fitting room a fur was wrapped around her shoulders, her hands were crossed over her breasts with the fur falling to the floor and she was wearing high heels as always. She said, "Do you like this?" and Travilla replied, "Fabulous!" He later revealed that, thanks to her position in front of the mirror, he could see her famously perfectly sculpted rear!

Marilyn Monroe was an actress in an era when the female body was hidden far more than it is today and yet her sensuality is unsurpassed. In the late 1980s Travilla, in an interview for the *LA Times*, spoke about nudity, words that are as true today as they were then. "Nudity? It has about run its course. We wear clothes for one reason now – to become more interesting. If you know everything, you've had it. Most women know that, so far as men are concerned, secrecy is the thing. It's an old saying that mystery, not diamonds, is a girl's best friend. With nudity allure vanishes. Nudity isn't disgusting, it's tiresome. It's incredible how intelligent people with small perspectives get uptight over temporary trends. Some of the toughest guys in history made love and war wearing skirts, tunics or kilts. Frankly attitudes about beards and busts bore me."

Marilyn did a lot of things to test people and Travilla was no exception. She was a tremendous exhibitionist but, because of her babyish quality, no one could resent it and there was nothing vulgar about her. She was adorable, using cute childish words and murmuring, "Oh goodness" in that unmistakable breathy voice. If criticized, she would give that Monroe giggle, and say, "Forgive me".

Travilla quickly became a close friend of Marilyn, once telling her, "Honey, you can do anything you want," and their relationship deepened to the point where she would not do a gallery sitting without him. It seemed that only he had the clothes and the eye to dress this beautiful girl. In one instance he remembered grabbing a piece of remnant satin, cutting a strip about 30 cm (12 inches) wide, then draping it on the bias straight onto her nude body, to evoke an evening gown held together with a rhinestone brooch falling into cascades to the floor. She looked more sensuous than any woman on earth and she suddenly became the Marilyn Monroe the world knew.

Despite her luminous appearance in films and in photographs, Travilla always thought Marilyn looked better in person. However wonderful she was on screen, the camera never really captured how truly beautiful she was because her features were too soft.

He also remembered the difference between the public face of Marilyn Monroe and the efforts she went to not to be recognized when going out in her private life. "There were two Marilyn Monroes. She never did anything without thinking about it first; she knew exactly what she wanted to achieve and she always got it. She was going to be seen by the public as the most exquisite, glamorous, magnificently beautiful movie star, or she would be seen as a slob, a slob to the point of putting lanolin on her face and hair, making it greasy. Later I learned by studying her closely. I said, 'You've got make-up on,' and she replied 'Of course I have.' She had a soft brownish-red outline to her lips, she had the strangest line of soft brown close to her lashes and rouge on her nose, cheeks and chin; it was a natural look and it was all covered with lanolin so you would swear she did not have a speck of make-up on. Despite the grease she was gorgeous.

"In her spotty jumpers and with her stringy hair we would go to lunch at the commissary at 20th Century Fox and she had her own table at the far end of the room, which meant we had to walk from the entrance all the way through the restaurant to the far end. I used to be very shy. I don't know why but I was and it was like walking a gangplank going to lunch with Marilyn as the whole room was looking at us. The studio broke at about the same time and it was crowded and it's a big, big place, you could hear the sound of cups and silverware and the whole room in conversation. There would be Bette Davis and Susan Hayward and all the current stars on our lot busy eating and talking and you'd see Bette Davis with her spoon half way to her mouth and then it stopped. Susan Hayward would stop in whatever position she was in. The waiters stopped. The whole place became silent, except muttering '...there she is,' and things like that. And that walk to me was like death because I knew that they knew who was walking with her too; I could feel my knees shake. And I remember she was wearing a pale jersey wraparound with giant cuffs and these big sleeves of ostrich feathers. The wrap was loose; it wrapped around her and tied at the waist. Under it was the naked body of Marilyn and the reaction was the same as if she was walking in naked except you couldn't see anything.

"On other occasions we went to lunch on Pico in LA for cheeseburgers and apple pie. It's a businessman's lunch place. She would be looking like my beautiful slob with dark glasses and a bandana covering her hair – luckily, as it looked awful underneath. There would be a line five deep waiting to get to the counter. One time she said: 'We'll never get out of here on time. Maybe I should take my glasses off.' I said, 'No! Everyone would recognize you and you are ugly.' And she giggled and we'd wait and get our cheeseburgers and go back to work."

Travilla had an affair with Marilyn, perhaps inevitably, given their close working relationship, and he described her magnetic qualities: "I adored her but I wasn't any different from any other man. No one could possibly go out with Marilyn Monroe and live through it without being in love. She had this incredible quality, a lovely quality, where, for example, if you went out with Marilyn to dinner

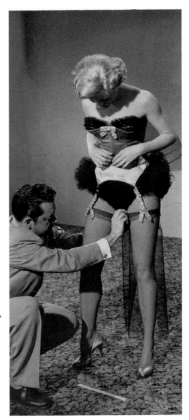

BELOW Travilla fixing Sheree North's costume.

AHEAD OF HER TIME

This photo, according to Bill Sarris, shows Monroe and Travilla with an unidentified African-American man at the 5-4 Club in south central Los Angeles in 1952. It has been in print only a handful of times, and has always appeared cropped, without the second man.

The story of this picture, as Travilla and Bill Sarris tell it, is that Travilla and Marilyn spent the evening at an almost exclusively black club in Los Angeles – something that just wasn't done in 1952. The studio was outraged, especially after the nude photograph scandal involving Marilyn in March of that year, and the fact that she had just been on the April cover of *Life* magazine and hailed as "The Talk of Hollywood". As a result of being "caught on camera", Travilla was fired from the film they were working on. But Marilyn – one of his closest friends – stood up and said, "If he goes, I go". Of course they let him stay, but they succeeded in keeping this picture out of the press.

Marilyn was ahead of her time in terms of racial equality and civil rights, claims Sarris. Even Ella Fitzgerald credited her with getting her into some of the "upper-crust" jazz clubs of the day.

BELOW An extremely rare photograph of Marilyn, Travilla and unidentified black man. At the time, the picture was cut down the middle and only the right-hand half used, never including the third man, as this was an age of racial segregation.

she looked only at you. If I was boring, which I presume I could be, she looked interested and she never looked at anyone else in the room. She just looked at you the entire time. You felt like a king, I felt six feet tall! And if we went dancing she would take her shoes off so we were the same height."

Part of Marilyn's appeal for Travilla, who often found himself overworked and up to his eyes in temperamental big stars, was that she took him back to the very early days of his career when everything was carefree and fun. Travilla sized Marilyn up from the beginning, describing her as "an untapped source of creative genius and completely natural with the instincts of a feral cat and the incandescent beauty that God seldom bestows on mere mortals". This, coupled with a drive and determination that equalled his own, convinced him that she would become a major star. He always made a point of giving her the respect she deserved for what it had taken to get so far and behaved impeccably towards her.

In the course of their working relationship Travilla created the costumes for eight of Marilyn's movies, including some of the most iconic and immediately recognizable of her dresses. He also designed many of her personal dresses, including adding rhinestone buttons and a fur collar to the outfit she wore to marry Joe DiMaggio in San Francisco in 1954. But by 1956 the monopolizing studio system was on the way out and 20th Century Fox declined to renew Travilla's contract as they cut back their in-house departments. This marked the end of his working relationship with Marilyn Monroe. The last film for which he designed her costumes was *Bus Stop* (1956), a true collaboration in which the actress and designer worked closely to achieve realistic costumes for the character of Cherie. The hard work paid off; Marilyn was praised for her performance and Travilla received another Oscar nomination for costume design.

Marilyn and Travilla remained friends almost to the end of her life. He went to see her on the set of her last film, *Something's Got to Give* (1962). She had laryngitis and told him it was stopping her working. He heard through the studio grapevine that she was causing problems but defended her as always, saying, "…but if she can't speak she can't act". He remembered hugging her and telling her that everything would be ok, but shortly after this meeting Fox shut down the film and Marilyn was asked to leave. The film was never completed.

The last time Travilla saw Marilyn was at Frascatti's, an upmarket Italian restaurant in Beverly Hills frequented by many of the glitterati. Travilla was having dinner with Bill Sarris, who recalls, "I saw a woman dressed in white with a matching turban. If she hadn't been so skinny and pale I would have sworn it was Marilyn Monroe." He dismissed it, until he heard the trademark childlike giggle. "That has to be Marilyn," he said, "no one else giggles like that."

Travilla excused himself and went over to say hello. Marilyn was having dinner with an English actor, Peter Lawford, and his wife and, to Travilla's shock, she did not recognize him for a second. As soon as she did, she was on her feet, hugging him. He remembered that she hugged him very tightly and he could not believe how skinny she was. He was understandably upset, and concerned about how she had acted – so much so that he was going to write to her to say how upset he was about her not recognizing him and, more importantly, to make sure she was ok. Sadly, he never wrote that letter, as a mere couple of days later Marilyn Monroe was found dead.

Travilla never believed she committed suicide, although he did not rule out her death being accidental. Revealingly, he commented that if she had died by her own hand she would have made a show of it – looking stunning in one of the negligées he made for her, all satin and ostrich feathers. She would have left this world the beautiful, voluptuous star she had always been in life.

After leaving 20th Century Fox, Travilla moved into fashion design and, with Sarris, launched the label Travilla, Inc. After relative job security as a contracted designer at 20th Century Fox, the move into fashion was tough, particularly as he was still working as a freelance costume designer for various studios. But his business-savvy partner Sarris was sure it would be a success, particularly with Travilla's little black book of impressive clients.

In an interview for *The New York Times* about designing for real women as well as movie characters, Travilla said: "There isn't much difference between the two. Let's face it, clothes are camouflage, clothes are meant to emphasize the good points and cover up the bad. And almost every person has some of each." A mark of his skill is that his clothes rarely looked as good on a hanger as they did on a woman. In fact, he was frustrated by women who thought clothes should look good when hanging up, admitting, "Many of my dresses don't. I design things to enhance the figure underneath. It's difficult to tell what the clothes will do for you while they're on a hanger. But women are getting out of the habit of trying things on unless they think they look good on the hanger. They are getting lazy and that means they're losing the chance to look better than they do. The glamorous film stars never decide until they have tried everything on."

In order to look her best, Travilla explained, a woman needs to see herself as a stranger might. In an interview for the *Cedar Rapids Gazette* in 1979 he remembered: "The brightest fashion woman I ever knew was Loretta Young. She had the ability of being Mrs Tom Lewis [referring to her husband] and then analyzing herself as Loretta Young in the mirror. She would look directly at me and say, 'Bill, I'm not sure I like Loretta,' or we would run screen tests of clothes and she would say, 'I'm not sure Loretta looks her best here. No, I don't think that's our girl,' and then discuss herself as if she were another person. What ability! She always looked right and she always was right." Travilla advised all women to try to do the same thing. "Be honest with yourself, look in the mirror and pretend the person you see is your best friend and you want her to look great." Advice of this sort, combined with his innate skill as a designer, helped the women he dressed to look magnificent on screen and off.

He went on to create a ready-to-wear line, which, thanks not only to his fashion-forward designs but also his inimitable charm and powers of persuasion, was snapped up by prestigious department store Neiman Marcus. The dresses reflected his signature style, using the famous sunburst pleats to create a timeless look. Travilla also continued designing for film and television, including for 1963's *The Stripper* (for which he received the last of his four Oscar nominations), for Diahann Carroll in *Julia* (a 1968–71 TV series) and for *Valley of the Dolls* (1967).

Alongside his costume-design career, his fashion business flourished throughout the US and Europe; the House of Travilla only closed its doors in 1995 after more than 40 years in business. Travilla took a break in the early 1970s when, disconcerted by '70s fashions after the elegance of the '50s and early '60s, he sold

ABOVE A costume test shot of Marilyn in the red one-piece swimsuit for *How to Marry a Millionaire* (1953). On all the test shots it states Des (designer) Travilla.

OPPOSITE The wedding day of Joe DiMaggio and Marilyn Monroe. Travilla added the fur collar and jewelled buttons to this suit.

his house in Hollywood. He moved to New York for eight months, then to La Manga del Mar Minor, a small resort in Murcia, Spain, where he recaptured his childhood days of swimming in the clear waters off Catalina Island. There he was known as the man who did alterations, not as a Hollywood designer.

In the spring of 1975 Bill Sarris arrived to drag Travilla back into designing and he resurfaced with a vengeance, working on his fashion label alongside Sarris and taking on more and more freelance costume design. One of the first design jobs he did was the television mini series *Moviola* in 1980. His first episode, called "This Year's Blonde", was dedicated to Marilyn Monroe's years as a struggling actress. The second, devoted to the stars of *Gone With the Wind*, was entitled "The Scarlet O'Hara Wars". For this he won his first Emmy. He found it amusing that his first foray back into costume design was based on the golden era of Hollywood, the period in which he had started out, noting, "Women wanted glamour again and I was able to give it to them."

His career hit a new high in the early 1980s with a series of costume designs as iconic in their way as those he had created for Marilyn's films. He was asked to redesign the look of the clothes in a show already airing on television: *Dallas*. Watching the series, Travilla was shocked to see that the supposedly glamorous characters were "wearing polyester". Thanks to a huge budget, he transformed them, making them more befitting their status as super-rich oil tycoons. Those strikingly designs helped the characters and the show achieve legendary status. Not only did Travilla win an Emmy for *Dallas*, but his designs for the show's female leads were credited with increasing the show's ratings.

Travilla also designed for many well-regarded TV mini-series in the '80s, including *The Thorn Birds*, *Evita Peron* and *The Jacqueline Bouvier Kennedy Story*. He relished designing for *Knots Landing* and for a show, set in a high-end department store, called *Berrenger's*. In this second part of his long and successful career as a costume designer he dressed a stream of stunning women, striking up friendships with many. These included Donna Mills, Linda Gray – whom he adored, saying, "she is as beautiful inside as she is outside" – and Sharon Tate, whom he declared "one of the nicest and most beautiful women I have ever met". He found them, like Marilyn, "a pleasure to dress". Travilla was nominated for an Emmy Award six years running (1980–86) and won twice, for "The Scarlett O'Hara Wars" episode of *Moviola* and for *Dallas*. He was nominated for an Oscar four times and won once. In the course of his career he dressed more than 200 stars and designed costumes for 120 movies and television shows, as well as creating hundreds of personal dresses for celebrity clients.

Aside from Travilla's enormous talent, his generosity of spirit earned him the great love of his friends, though not of rival designers. A good friend of his the lovely Bunny Seidman, told me how, at a Hollywood New Year's Eve party in 1956, she had worn a head-turning red gown lent to her by Travilla. He had created it for Loretta Young for *The Loretta Young Show* on TV. Bunny was very nervous about wearing the dress but Travilla, being a generous man, insisted. "He said he did not need it any more for the rushes, so I thought it would be ok."

Although Travilla was not at the party, a fellow Hollywood costume designer, Orry-Kelly, was. According to Bunny, "Kelly hated Travilla and constantly accused him of stealing Kelly's designs. He came over to me and said, 'that's the

OPPOSITE AND BELOW A beautiful sketch of the stunning Loretta Young in a dress Travilla designed for her TV show.

" *Billy Dear,*
Please dress me
forever. I love you. **"**

Marilyn

most gorgeous gown I have ever seen. Did Michael Novarese do it?' When I told him Travilla did it, he spilled his drink all over me. It was a disaster. I called Travilla next morning to tell him what had happened and he said they needed to reshoot Loretta's entrance and he needed the gown back as soon as possible. He told me to take it to a specific dry cleaner, so, incredibly hung over, I jumped in my car and headed to the cleaners, but they would not touch it. I was hysterical by this point. Finally, Travilla, always calm, called his dressmakers in to work; it was a Saturday if I remember correctly. They had to completely re-do it identically for that afternoon. They saved my skin. Of course I didn't tell him that I had also slept in it."

William Travilla died on 2 November 1990 in Los Angeles at the age of 70. He left a legacy of a remarkable archive of costumes spanning five decades of fashion and costume design. So much was this work his identity that in an interview he once said, "When I die, don't have me cremated, have me pleated."

OPPOSITE Marilyn and Travilla in a publicity shot for *Gentlemen Prefer Blondes*.

LEFT An article written about Travilla in March 1990, just eight months before he passed away. The photo at top left of the article is the cropped one from the club shown on page 45 of this book.

The Red Dress

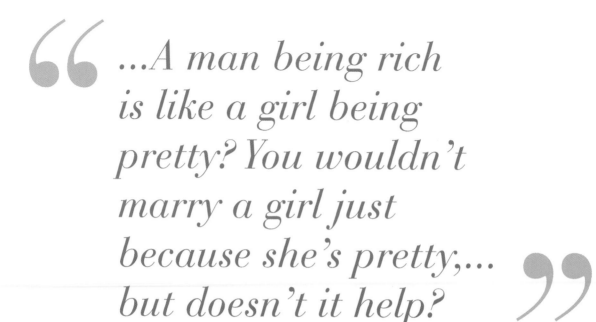

> *...A man being rich is like a girl being pretty? You wouldn't marry a girl just because she's pretty,... but doesn't it help?*

All the costumes in the movie *Gentleman Prefer Blondes* (1953) were created in vivid jewel tones, colours that Marilyn always wore for her on-screen persona, although ironically in real life her own clothes were the total opposite. The opening scene sets the tone for the entire movie. On a stage in a nightclub appear two girls, one blonde and one brunette, bursting through black, sheer, glittery curtains, wearing striking red and singing the catchy tune "Two Little Girls from Little Rock".

Those two girls were Marilyn Monroe and Jane Russell. Physically, their colouring was in stark contrast but in this scene they wore matching costumes. It was a difficult job for Travilla as their bodies and heights were very different. However, by choosing such a vivid red, he managed to design a dress that suited them both beautifully.

As the opening credits rolled Jane Russell and Marilyn Monroe stepped on to the stage, throwing white fur coats lined in the same fabric as the dresses into the audience and breaking into that famous dance number. The dresses sparkled as if they were covered in rubies – the ultimate showgirl costumes.

Everything in costume design is done for a reason. Opening with such a strong colour excites the eye and guides you into the movie. If the movie had opened with the pink dress in which Marilyn sang "Diamonds Are A Girl's Best Friend" (see pages 70–88), it would not have had the same impact. The costumes, like the script, tell a story, even if we don't recognize it – that is the genius of the costume designer.

This dress is definitely a statement piece. There were a lot of showgirl costumes in the movie and this dress is sometimes overlooked when people talk about the film, but it really stands out. Its colour and form-fitting shape positively ooze sex appeal on screen. Of all the costumes in the movie this really shows Marilyn and Jane as the showgirls they are.

PAGE 50 Marilyn Monroe and Jane Russell in the opening scene of *Gentlemen Prefer Blondes*.

OPPOSITE The costume test shot of Marilyn in the "Little Rock" costume. Notice the differences in the prototype and the dress worn on screen.

698 - HAWKS
MARILYN
MONROE
AS
LORELEI LEE

Weddings Seq.
Jag

Don Traville
1-13-53

The dresses themselves are made of a heavy crepe fabric, lined in crepe, with thousands of hand-sewn sequins spiralling in every direction. This allows them to catch the light from all angles. A deep split to high above the thigh, caught by a diamond brooch, added to the drama of this dress. The slightly risqué bust area once again fooled the censors by including a sheer body-toned fabric from the neck right down to the waist, which gave the impression of nudity without actually being revealing. There was also Travilla's trademark V-shaped boning from the waist to just below the bust to keep the shape and the sheer fabric taut.

OPPOSITE The original red sequin dress from *Gentlemen Prefer Blondes*. This dress, previously owned by Debbie Reynolds, fetched $1.2 million when it was sold at auction in June 2011.

LEFT Marilyn and Jane in a publicity shot for *Gentlemen Prefer Blondes*.

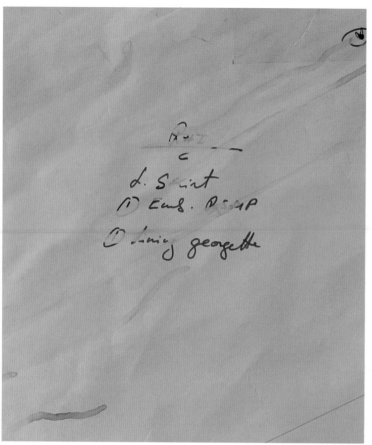

The jewellery was all added separately after the dress was completed. Last year I met a lovely lady in Palm Springs who told me this revealing anecdote: "I used to work for Travilla as a runner in his studio when I was around 18 years old. This would mean I would go out and buy bits and pieces that they might need, like jewellery. I remember that dress being made as I thought it was so beautiful. I was also there for most of Marilyn's fittings. During this time I was asked to go into LA to buy some costume jewellery. I came back with the earrings." She told me the earrings cost about $2.50.

"After shooting Marilyn gave me the earrings which I still have and I bet they're worth more than $2.50 now!" she said. "I'm not sure if Marilyn was supposed to give something that belonged to the studio away but, who cares, it shows what a kind lady she was."

To finish the look a hat was worn: a skull cap of matching sequins, with red and white feathers starting on one side of the face and wrapping around to the other. As with many of Travilla's designs, there was another version of the outfit which involved a hat similar to a trident, with feathers sticking out from either side, along with white feathers coming out from behind the brooch at the top of the split. Both the initial hat design and the white feathers were rejected.

ABOVE RIGHT Travilla's sketch for the red dress. Along with the sketch for the purple dress (see pages 88–101), the original is currently missing from The Travilla Estate.

ABOVE LEFT This is part of the red dress pattern, detailing that the lining was made of georgette.

OPPOSITE The original pattern to the costume. At some point a photocopy of Marilyn and Jane was placed over the original pencil drawing. This shows that Travilla used the pattern for one of his couture dresses. Patterns were always revisited. All these patterns survived a flood and fire and show damage in places.

for show
special

Embroidery from India (georgette   send fab with Mercer!
② F. Bodice
② B. Bodice
② Sleeve
① R. Skt.
① L. Skt

Lining (georgette
② F. Bodice
② B. Bodice
① R. Skt. lining
① L. Skt.
Bias for neck and sleeve piping
   1¾ x 3yd.

Canvs.
① C.F. Insert.

Organza (Red)
② F. Inter   ① R. skt Inter
② S. Inter   ① L. Skt Inter
① waist stay

Paper. Shape
① F. & Neck Shape.

Chiffon (Red
② sleeve

The Gold Dress

Thanks to its revealing design and the unfortunate coincidence of the negative publicity generated by her appearance nude in a calendar, Marilyn Monroe failed to wear the original diamonds dress that Travilla designed for her in the movie *Gentlemen Prefer Blondes* (1953) (*see* pages 72–75). However a second, equally revealing dress that did appear in the film, albeit briefly, was the gold lamé dress and, ironically, it is this pleated sheath, slashed to the waist, that has become one of the most popular images of the iconic actress.

How Marilyn managed to wear it without attracting the attention of the censors, even for that brief moment, is still a mystery. The dress is only visible from the back for a few seconds in a ballroom scene where Jane Russell is looking at Marilyn through the widow but even in that short time it is obvious that it radiates sex appeal. In fact, this dress, just like the original diamonds dress, was scripted to appear in several scenes but was cut from most of them as, once again, the censors did not feel it appropriate. However even with the censors' ban this provocative dress was to boost Marilyn's popularity immensely.

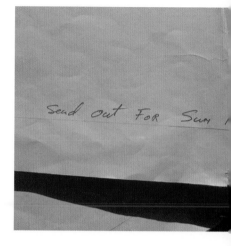

ABOVE Part of the patten circle stating "send out for sun burst pleating".

LEFT The short scene showing Marilyn as Lorelei dancing in the ballroom with Lord Beekman. This is the only time this dress is shown in the movie.

OPPOSITE The original pattern to the gold lamé dress. Again, a photocopy replaces the original image. This pattern is one complete circle of paper. The lining has more pieces.

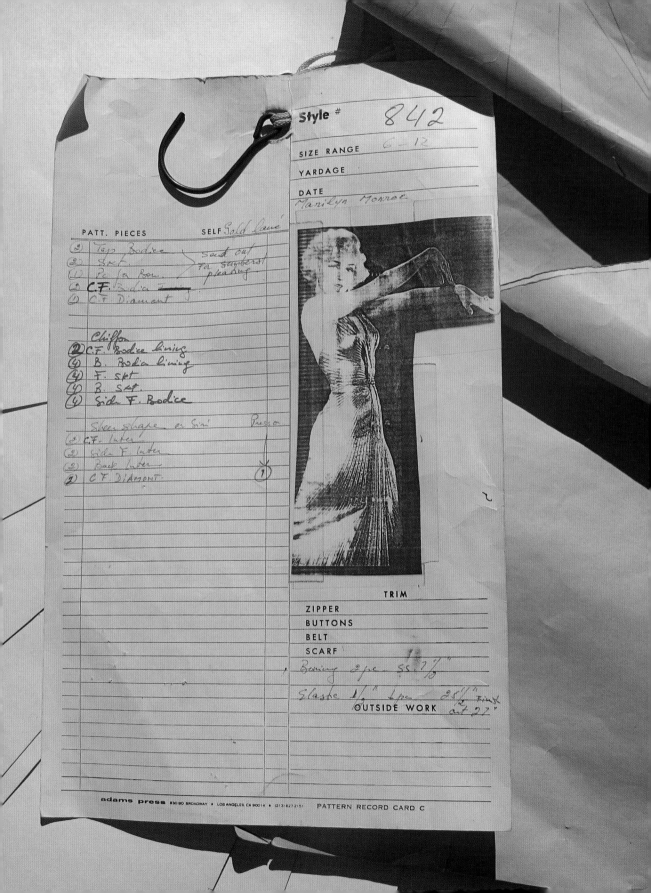

Style # 842

SIZE RANGE   6 - 12

YARDAGE

DATE

Marilyn Monroe

PATT. PIECES   SELF *Gold Lamé*

(2) Top Bodice   Sold out
(2) Sk.f.   for sunburst
(1) P. f. Bow.   pleating
(2) C.F. Bodice Lining
(2) C.F. Diamant

Chiffon
(2) C.F. Bodice lining
(4) B. Bodice lining
(4) F. Skt.
(4) B. Skt.
(4) Side F. Bodice

Sheer shape or Siri   Presser
(2) C.F. Inter.
(2) Side F. Inter
(2) Back Inter
(2) C.F. Diamant.   (1)

TRIM

ZIPPER
BUTTONS
BELT
SCARF
, Boning 2 pc. ss 7½"
Elastic 1½" 4 pc. 25½" first
OUTSIDE WORK   cut 27"

Although the censors were formidably keen in ensuring that no excessive flesh was revealed by a movie actress, good designers like Travilla knew how to push them to the limit without breaking the rules – rules that seem ridiculous to us today, when modern designers regularly push an actress's bust in, up and almost out! In the 1950s you were not allowed to show even a shadow of a cleavage, though many would argue that there is much to be said for the less-is-more approach. Travilla used to say that Marilyn "…had the best breasts in Hollywood," not, as you might think, thanks to their size or pertness but for the fact that they were naturally quite far apart allowing him to create dresses slashed to the waist without having to put in excessive boning to push them apart, a trick achieved today by using tape.

Travilla's incredible attention to detail and construction methods never failed to impress and this dress is no exception. Created out of a single complete circle of particular gold lamé (a fabric no longer available) and sunburst pleated, this dress was a designer's dream. If the dress is viewed closely, it is possible to see that every pleat lines up perfectly along the back seam. It has two thin, inflexible iron bars in a v-shape, starting at the waist and traveling up to the bust thus moulding the dress to Marilyn's body.

It might be said that Travilla's trademark is his use of sunburst pleating. Tucked away on W. Third Street in Los Angeles is an incredible shop called A-1 pleating. It has been around for years and the owners remember Travilla well. They are still very successful but love to talk about the past and will regale you with stories of the glorious days when couture was paramount and everything was handmade. This was a time when designers came in personally showing designs that, at first glance, seemed impossible. Travilla's intricate designs were a case in point. Occasionally someone new to the shop would ask where the shop's machines were located and the owner would simply show them his hands.

There are many tricks a costume designer can employ when manipulating fabrics and materials in order to achieve the perfect design and the art of pleating is one. It is a method that dates back to the ancient Egyptians and Greeks, an era that Travilla loved but pleats are actually the Japanese technique of giving an accordion-like configuration to any kind of material.

A pleat describes when fabric is secured at one edge and released at the other. Pleats are first sewn and can be set using heat, steam and pressure. At one time fabric was always pleated by hand but later pleats were more commonly created by a mechanical process and then heated in order to make the structure of the pleats permanent. The pleating machine has an array of hundreds of needles that grab the fabric; the wheel is then manually turned to create them. A straight pleat is relatively easy to achieve. However a sunburst pleat is quite different – complex and extremely beautiful as a series of evenly spaced, radiating, alternating creases create a raised and recessed pattern.

The love Travilla had for the sunburst pleat is obvious when you look through the archives of his estate, which houses many varying versions of this design. Some are in silk with a beaded front, others in chiffon with a single dropped jewel open just below the cleavage. Each one is exquisite in its manufacture, a work of pure genius. Part of the reason Travilla loved this design so much is that it complemented most women's figures, in fact the curvier the

OPPOSITE That famous pout, in that famous dress.

better. And as Travilla always emphasized he liked to dress "women" not stick insects.

The gold dress was so figure-hugging that Marilyn had to be sewn into it for her brief yet noteworthy appearance, although as the dress had no fixed lining she wore a separate under-slip. Despite its obvious success, the dress did cause Travilla some problems with the lovely Marilyn, as he recalled in an interview for the *Los Angeles Times* in 1979, saying "back in 1952 she succeeded in driving me absolutely mad over that dress!"

Marilyn clearly loved the dress, and she intended to wear it when accepting an award at the 1953 Photoplay awards hosted at the Beverly Hills Hotel in Los Angeles. Initially Travilla refused, recalling that: "It was fine for the movie, but for real life it was way too sexy and flashy. Also it was never completed as it didn't even have a zipper".

When Marilyn called him up after the film had finished shooting and asked him to get the dress out of the wardrobe department so that she could wear it for this particular event, the designer was horrified, warning her, "absolutely not, it is totally inappropriate". She kept on calling and begging him, but Travilla would not give in until a call arrived from a laughing Marilyn telling him that Darryl Zanuck, the head of 20th Century Fox told her to tell him, to "unlock the dress and give her what she wants." Once again Marilyn got her way.

Travilla was furious that Marilyn had gone over his head; sweet and childish one moment she became coquettish and manipulative the next in order to get what she wanted. After some discussion he finally agreed that she could wear the dress with a few adjustments. The first was that she would keep her hair simple and wear little jewellery. She refused, however, to wear any under-slip and was once again sewn into the dress, although she promised him that she would walk like a lady, which obviously meant that she would lose the trademark Marilyn wiggle. According to Travilla she kept her promise but with that dress on it made very little difference – a serious scandal was inevitable.

In the audience that evening was the outspoken Joan Crawford whose obvious jealousy may well have been the reason for her unkind comment. "She looks vulgar", she was quoted as saying. However Marilyn knew exactly what she was doing that night. She was the queen of self-publicity and knew exactly how to work the press and give her fans what they really wanted. When she pushed her bottom out to the side as she leaned over to kiss the host, photographers mobbed the stage, snide comments from other onlookers quickly forgotten. As the sensational photograph hit the front page of newspapers around the globe a sex symbol was born.

To this day, the picture of Marilyn wearing the gold lamé gown is one of the most used photographs of her, along with the shot of her standing astride a subway grate, dress blowing up in the wind, from *The Seven Year Itch* (1955). Both these pictures show the actress at her most provocative, albeit for very different reasons – the white dress because of the revealing way in which it blew up and the gold dress for how it allowed Marilyn's natural sexuality to shine through.

Travilla later commented, "that was the first and last time I tried to tell Marilyn what to do. She always knew best and when it came to her image she always got her way with the public and the press".

When it came to public opinion, Marilyn could do no wrong. With any other star the controversy surrounding the nude calendar or wearing this sensational dress would have been a disaster, but not for Marilyn; with her everything she did that might have gone wrong always paid off. It was Marilyn's fans that made her a star not the studio. And those fans young and old are still out there in their thousands; 50 years after her death she is bigger than ever.

As with other Travilla's designs, there was more than one version of this gold dress and there is some confusion as to which design Marilyn actually wore in *Gentlemen Prefer Blondes*. Travilla created three versions: one with a belt, one with four golden balls in the centre of the waist and another with a bow. In the test shot for the movie she wore the belted dress, but neither Travilla nor Marilyn liked this version and she never wore it. She did, however, wear the version with the golden balls, as can be seen in the publicity photos on pages 63, 64 and 67. Marilyn may have worn this version in the movie or the one with the bow. As the dress is only seen from the back, we will never know, but the actress's favourite version was the one with the bow. During his career Travilla created many versions of this dress – always with a bow, which tells us that he preferred this version too.

ABOVE Marilyn wearing the gold lamé gown to accept an award at the 1953 *Photoplay* awards hosted at the Beverly Hills Hotel in Los Angeles.

OPPOSITE A stunning publicity shot of Marilyn in one of the most famous dresses created for her.

Marilyn never wore this dress design again but Travilla used it for plenty of other stars. Jayne Mansfield wore it, complete with the golden balls, in the movie *The Spirit of St. Louis* in 1957, and Betty Grable wore the belted version in a TV special in 1954 called *A Shower of Stars*.

There is no doubt that this dress has become synonymous with glamour and sex appeal – in fact, it earned Travilla the title of "The Man Who Dressed Sex Symbols". To create a dress like this you have to think from the inside out and, although the design appears simple, the structure is incredibly complicated and has left many people frustrated.

Needless to say, there have been many copies of Marilyn's most famous dresses – particularly the white dress from *The Seven Year Itch* – but I have seen only a few copies of the gold dress and all were a disaster. All Travilla's dresses are very hard to copy. Even the copy of the pink diamonds dress that Madonna wore in her "Material Girl" video wasn't close to being accurate. Without thorough research and careful recreation it is impossible to produce a replica of any of Travilla's dresses.

Over the years many people have asked to borrow the patterns for Travilla's designs or to inspect the dresses up close as they wanted to reproduce them, but I have always said no for two reasons: either their interest was purely financial or they simply would not have done the dresses justice. Last year, however, I was asked by Suzie Kennedy, one of the leading Marilyn Monroe look-alikes and someone I count as a close friend and supporter of the Travilla exhibitions, if I knew anyone who would be able to make her a copy of the gold lamé dress. When Suzie "becomes" Marilyn she does it with such respect and dignity that I was more than willing to help.

A year or so before I had been to see a man called Kevin Freeman of Renaissance Creative Design in Brighton, who had been getting rave reviews in the press and who created designs that I really liked. I went to him with a dress badly in need of repair to get his opinion on what I should do. He still laughs now at my naïvety, recalling that, "to my amusement and horror he produced out of a gym bag a dress created for Judy Garland that is incredibly heavy and covered in beads."

Of course, as Kevin did not know me at the time he was very polite about my gym bag and told me what I needed to know and I have obviously since placed the dress in an appropriate garment bag! When Suzie asked me if I knew someone to make a copy of the gold dress I instantly thought of Kevin. I took Travilla's gold lamé dress with me, nervous that for the first time a designer was going to be able to see how this dress was constructed. However, I needn't have worried as he did a wonderful job.

I recently asked Kevin exactly how he went about re-creating this legendary dress as it is fascinating to realize the intricacy of its design. His first issue was the fabric, because, he said, "the fabric of the original dress was antique gold with a very soft drape, which is incredibly important with this dress. It was also a complete circle of sunray-pleated fabric radiating from a central point at the waist. Contemporary lamé is very stiff with little drape so an alternative is liquid lamé, a knitted and foiled fabric which potentially has the drape but no 'body'."

Having asked for endless samples, which were the right colour but wrong fabric or right fabric but wrong colour, Kevin finally decided on paper lamé as being the closest fabric and colour to the original. Although it is stiffer than the

OPPOSITE A closer view of Marilyn wearing the gold dress which shows how well it fitted her curves.

original, it would hold the pleat and photograph in a similar way. Essentially the problem lay in the fact that the original was only created for the movie and was never really meant to last. This copy was to be a costume that had to travel well and maintain its shape with Suzie's many performances.

For the pleating, Kevin explained, "I always use Ciment Pleaters. They are based in Potters Bar and are one of the few remaining traditional pleaters in the UK. They produce the majority of pleated work for the UK for clients as diverse as fashion designers, international couturiers and film costume designers as well as performers such as Lady Gaga. Their patterns and templates date back up to 80 years."

He also explains the process they use in creating the pleats: "All templates are hand-scored and hand-folded onto two sheets of card. The bottom layer of pleated card is stretched flat on a cutting table using weights and clamps. The cut fabric is laid on top of the template. The corresponding layer of card is laid on top and the weights released. The 'pleated' fabric and card templates are clamped together and placed in the steam room. The steam 'sets' the pleats'". When starting the design for the copy Kevin explains: "Initially, I had two 3 metre (3.2 yards) diameter semi circles of gold paper lamé 'sunray' pleated. But first the fabric shrank and tightened slightly giving me less drop to work with and second I realized that because the fabric was 112cm (44 inches) wide, the greatest distance in the dress was from front waist to centre back and the initial drape was too short. This meant I had to change the apex of the pleat from the centre of the semi-circle to roughly two thirds across the diameter and also add a panel to the longest section. This worked and I had two sets of fabric pleated, one for the 'toile' and one for the final piece".

When I asked Kevin about the process of construction he answered: "The original had a soft mesh lining with a v-shaped metal bar from the waist upwards to the bust to support the neckline and stop it gaping. I built this dress over a soft cotton jersey 'mount' which was darted and fitted Suzie like a glove. This stopped at thigh length and concealed the specially made flexisteel support. This gave me something with a bit of 'give' on which to work the straight grain and bias of the pleats over Suzie's body but which would also give substance

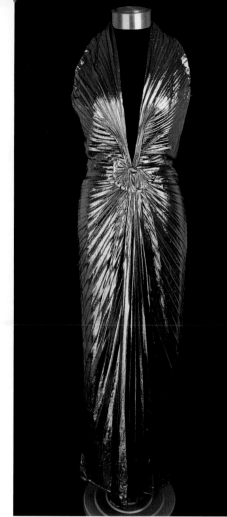

ABOVE Travilla's prototype for the gold lamé dress, which was incredibly difficult to make.

FAR LEFT The bodice of the gold dress in which intricate pleating and iron bars support the bust line.

LEFT A close-up of the hem of the dress. The fabric is impossible to find now and a lot of care is needed to look after it.

to the paper lamé to stop it shredding. The position of the straight grain and the bias is essential to achieve the fit around the body. With no darts or side seams, the fabric tells you where it wants to go to fit the body. The bias has to move over the fullness of the bust and the swell of the hip to achieve the fit. Despite padding the stand, I still had to move and tack in place the majority of the pleats at Suzie's second fitting to accommodate a living figure".

Kevin worked on an original couture mannequin from the 1950s to "place" the pleats. The proportions of the mannequin include a small waist to hip ratio and a high bust (just as Marilyn and Suzie both have) but he still needed to pad the bust to achieve the right figure.

He also explained "There is a common misconception that all the pleats radiate from the waist… they don't. A good fit around the ribcage and under the bust is achieved by shaping the straight grain pleats from centre back to centre front and hand-sewing them in place to the jersey mount. The hand-sewing is then disguised by the straight grain drape which runs from waist to centre back neck to achieve the halter neck. All the other drapes are then caught into the centre front waist, which is disguised with the pleated bow detail".

In the original dress the softness of the fabric allowed an "Egyptian" drape from the waist to floor to add fullness to the skirt but Kevin could not achieve exactly the same mainly because paper lamé is very stiff and stuck out at the front when trying to achieve a drape, even when hand sewn in place. For Suzie's purposes it was perfect as she wanted the dress to be even closer fitting than the original but it illustrates both the complexity and relative fragility of the dress Marilyn wore and why no-one has managed to replicate it since. Finally the dress was lined with a full-length silky, stretch nylon for comfort and to try and suggest the lightness of the original despite it having the jersey mount.

The finished result is stunning. The adaptation is as brilliant as it is complex and even with the constraints Kevin faced I am sure his final result would have made Travilla very happy.

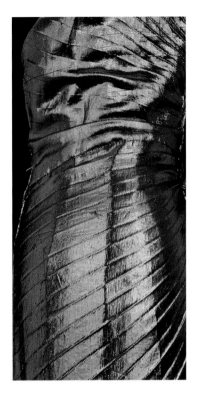

ABOVE This photograph illustrates the seamless pleats and the gathering which meet at the front of the dress.

LEFT The bow on the dress. This version of the dress was Marilyn and Travilla's favourite.

Travilla

The Pink Dress

"Diamonds Are a Girl's Best Friend"– this famous line is, of course, the title of a song and dance routine in the movie *Gentleman Prefer Blondes* (1953), performed brilliantly by Marilyn Monroe. It is by far the best interpretation of a scene so memorable that, over the years, many – including Madonna, Geri Halliwell and Kylie Minogue – have tried to re-enact it. However, no imitation ever comes close to the original performance of the song, which was listed as the twelfth-most-important movie song of all time by the American Film Institute in 2007.

Gentlemen Prefer Blondes is a much-loved and incredibly popular movie from the golden age of Hollywood, which saw Marilyn Monroe and her co-star in the film, Jane Russell, become household names across America and indeed

OPPOSITE A costume test shot of the dress originally designed to be worn for the number "Diamonds Are a Girl's Best Friend" which was later replaced by the pink dress.

LEFT A back view costume test shot of the original dress. So much detail and work went into this costume.

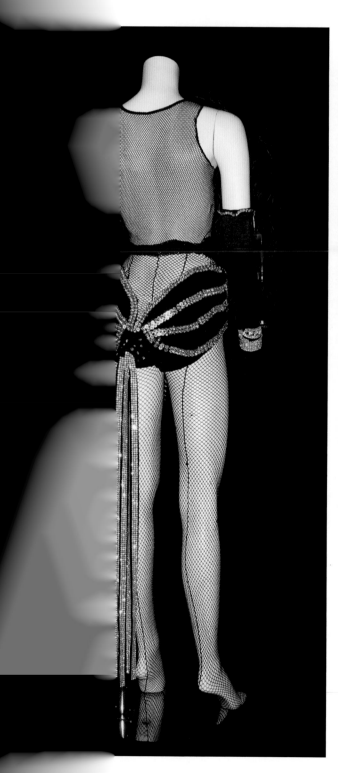

ABOVE The front view of the diamonds costume complete with the large brooch and dangling diamonds.

LEFT A back view of the bottom piece of the diamonds costume now. The stunning diamond tail trails to the floor.

ABOVE A detail of the costume – these images are courtesy of Greg Schreiner who now owns this dress.

TOP LEFT A close-up view of the bottom of the diamonds dress. The weight of this part of the costume is incredible as the stones are large and there are many of them.

LEFT The side view of the diamonds that travelled around the hips to the tail behind.

world. At the time of making *Gentleman Prefer Blondes* Jane Russell was already a huge star and Marilyn Monroe was yet to achieve the status of legendary Hollywood icon, yet the two actresses became friends, with Russell describing Monroe as shy and sweet but also much more intelligent that most people thought.

Russell later recalled that Monroe showed her dedication by rehearsing her dance routines each evening after most of the crew had left, although she arrived habitually late on set for filming. Realizing that Monroe remained in her dressing room through stage fright and that director Howard Hawks was growing impatient with her tardiness, Russell started escorting her to the set. It has been said many times that Marilyn was "just the blonde" in the movie and Jane Russell the star, yet Jane welcomed Monroe at once and gained her confidence professionally and personally. In Marilyn's last interview with *Life* magazine,

conducted just two days before her death in August 1962, she recalled that Russell "was quite wonderful to me".

This film was Monroe's big breakout role and is a movie that made her a worldwide icon of the big screen and secured her place in Hollywood's most exclusive halls of fame. Looking at the film even now, so many years after its release, it's easy to see why. Everything about this film sparkles – and that's not just because of its vibrant colour. The script, the acting and the musicality are all aspects that contribute to the movie's outstanding success.

In *Gentleman Prefer Blondes* Marilyn's character, Lorelei Lee, is being followed on an ocean liner by a detective hired by her fiancé's father. He is told of compromising pictures taken with a diamond-mine owner and cancels her credit before she arrives in France, forcing her to work in a Paris nightclub to survive. Her fiancé arrives just in time to see her perform "Diamonds Are A Girl's Best Friend".

ABOVE LEFT Although this costume was not worn by Marilyn Monroe in Gentlemen Prefer Blondes, the top portion was used in another film, How To Be Very, Very Popular (1955), worn by Sheree North. Unfortunately, all that remains today of the original costume is the bottom half and the ostrich-feather fan. This part of the costume is owned by Greg Schreiner.

OPPOSITE Marylin wearing the famous pink dress in the "Diamonds Are a Girl's Best Friend" scene.

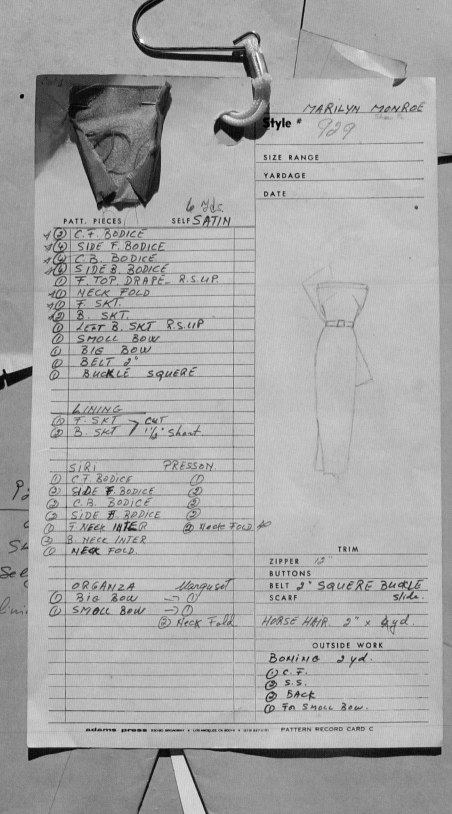

MARILYN MONROE Show Pc

Style # 929

SIZE RANGE _____

YARDAGE _____

DATE _____

6 Yds.

PATT. PIECES   SELF SATIN

✓② C.F. BODICE
✓④ SIDE F. BODICE
✓④ C.B. BODICE
✓④ SIDE B. BODICE
① F. TOP. DRAPE — R.S. UP.
①① NECK FOLD
✓① F. SKT.
✓② B. SKT.
① LEFT B. SKT R.S. UP
① SMALL BOW
① BIG BOW
① BELT 2"
① BUCKLE SQUERE

_____

LINING
① F. SKT ⟶ CUT
② B. SKT ⟶ 1½" Short.

_____

SIRI   PRESSON.
① C.F. BODICE   ①
③ SIDE F. BODICE   ②
② C.B. BODICE   ②
② SIDE B. BODICE   ②
① F. NECK INTER   ② Necke FOLD ⚹
② B. NECK INTER
① NECK FOLD.

_____

ORGANZA   Marquset
① BIG BOW   ⟶ ①
① SMALL BOW ⟶ ①
             ② Neck Fold

TRIM

ZIPPER 12"
BUTTONS
BELT 2" SQUERE BUCKLE
SCARF   slide.

HORSE HAIR. 2" × 4yd.

OUTSIDE WORK

BONING 2yd.
① C.F.
② S.S.
② BACK
① For SMALL BOW.

adams press 8030 BROADWAY • LOS ANGELES, CA 90014 • (213) 627-2191   PATTERN RECORD CARD C

P_
_____
F. SK___
① Sel___
① linie___

The film was a great vehicle for Marilyn. The dance routines allowed her to show off her sensuality as she swung her hips in a way that no performer has quite managed to emulate and, just as importantly, it cemented her ability at incredible comic timing. Lastly, it is memorable for showing the actress in some of the most beautiful gowns created for any movie, thanks, of course, to William Travilla.

This was a dream project for Travilla to work on, dressing two beautiful women with an unlimited budget and complete artistic control. It had its challenges, as Marilyn and Jane were very different in their look and stature, and in a few of the scenes he had to create the same dress while showing of their individual assets, but he pulled it off beautifully. In the famous opening sequence, when they perform "Two Little Girls from Little Rock", it is impossible to make a judgement on who looks better as they both look equally amazing

ABOVE One of the two sketches created by Travilla for the second "Diamonds Are A Girl's Best Friend" costume.

OPPOSITE The original pattern for the pink dress with the original fabric attached in the top left corner. This pattern is in good condition. Travilla never drew on the pattern information sheet, the cutters did that.

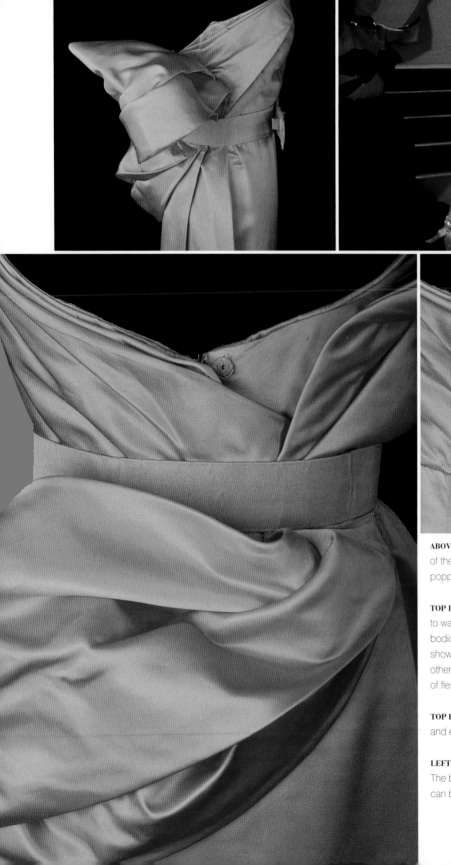

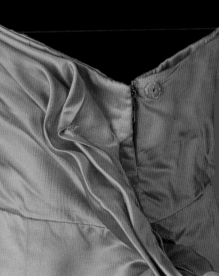

ABOVE This image shows the three layers of the bodice in detail, plus the hand sewn poppers of which there are eight.

TOP LEFT The unusual darting from mid breast to waist. Under this dart is more boning. This bodice will not move an inch. This picture also shows the first layer being higher than the others which stopped any unsightly overhang of flesh.

TOP RIGHT The finished bow. After a lot of trial and error a black lining was added to the bow.

LEFT A close-up look at Travilla's prototype. The bow is stuffed with horse hair and wire and can be manipulated by hand.

However, while this movie was in development, no one could envision the shocking revelations that were about to unfold, causing untold pressure for Travilla. It is this story of the design, or rather designs, for the dress that Marilyn Monroe wore when performing her legendary song that is most extraordinary and illustrates Travilla's skill and resourcefulness to the full.

The original design for the actress to wear to sing "Diamonds Are A Girl's Best Friend" was very different from the one that eventually found its way onto the screen. In his first sketches Travilla created a dream costume for one of the most sensuous women he had ever known. The base of the design was a fishnet body stocking that would travel up her body as far as her breasts, which would be covered in nude fabric. An incredibly ornate necklace of diamonds started across her shoulders and cascaded down into a huge brooch just below her breasts. The bottom was a velvet virtual harness with very large hooks that kept it in place on her hips. Finally, four strands of giant stones travelled around her hips to the front, then flowed down into more jewels. At the back the dress pulled into five floor-length pieces of velvet covered in diamonds to represent a tail plunging down. The headdress was more diamonds, a tiara with a black bird of paradise and black gloves. This original costume was incredibly ornate and cost close to $4,000. A local jeweller secured the jewels directly onto the dress as Marilyn wore it. This took hours but was very important as the stones had to be placed perfectly so they would not turn and catch on the fishnet hose.

Sadly, this incredible dress was never to grace the silver screen or, at least not with Marilyn Monroe wearing it, thanks to a scandal that came straight out of Marilyn's past. During post-production of the movie a calendar hit the streets causing horror to the studio directors. Marilyn had posed nude for this calendar, entitled "Golden Dreams", in May 1949 after Fox did not renew her contract; she was out of work and desperately needed the money. Marilyn was paid a mere $50 for this shoot, which was the exact amount she needed to get her impounded car released.

When the calendar made its appearance several years later the studio went crazy; they thought they would lose all their investment in the movie. She was called to the studio and admitted she had done a calendar years before but argued how could it hurt? They said, "It can hurt!"

TOP LEFT Marilyn striking a pose in "Diamonds Are a Girl's Best Friend".

TOP RIGHT A detail of the belt. It is leather with the pink silk glued to it.

RIGHT The original concept for the new dress included black gloves and shoes, and no one is sure why they became pink, but Travilla redid his sketch to show pink gloves. When people see the actual dress they often remark that in real life is lighter than it appears in the movie. That is easily explained by the use of glorious Technicolor. According to Travilla himself, not only did he have to design the dress, but he had to make sure he got the fabric right, as Technicolor would make it appear more vibrant on film.

Travilla

In fact, the one person it hurt most was Travilla, who, although the movie went ahead, had to completely redesign her costumes. His orders were simply: "Cover her up, we are not selling her body." So the original diamonds dress, an amazing work of art that had taken months in preparation, not to mention the fact that, from a design point of view, it would have fitted perfectly with the song, was dumped. And it was back to the drawing board for Travilla.

A new gown had to be created and in a matter of hours Travilla came up with the glorious pink concoction that is now synonymous with this musical number. But the problem remained, how does one create a gown that covers everything but still shows sensuality and allowed Marilyn to move?

Travilla chose a silk satin called *peau d'ange*, a fabric now rarely used, to realize his vision of a strapless, pale-pink, figure-hugging gown that showed all Marilyn's curves and, more importantly, was comfortable and flexible enough to allow her the freedom of movement that would be needed for such a complicated dance number. All this without showing anything that might remind the moviegoers of her recent scandalous photographs.

This gown was created, in Travilla's words, as "an envelope design", with few seams or darts; it was folded into shape on her body with a hidden zip in the centre and the fabric wrapping to the right side of the body, finally being fixed by six handmade, matching cotton poppers that held the dress in place. Finally, a matching belt was added. Of course, a strapless dress made in this way would look great when standing still, but there was a problem when it came to going up and down stairs. Travilla wanted to make sure there would be no creases in the skirt, which proved almost impossible with a dress like this but he managed it.

After a lot of trial and error with finding a lining stiff enough to add structure to the fluid silk satin, he came up with the idea of felt. The silk satin was glued directly to the felt – the same iron-stiff felt that would be used on a billiard table – then a black silk lining was added over the felt to match the bow and it wa

ABOVE LEFT Marilyn at the start of her famous routine.

ABOVE RIGHT This shows the "envelope" design Travilla did for this dress, as well as the complex and intricate back.

wrapped around Marilyn, beautifully keeping its shape. As Travilla described it, "I took a brilliant candy-pink silk *peau d'ange* made in Paris and flattened that to a green billiard felt with an overlay of silk. Apart from the two side seams the dress was folded into shape rather like cardboard. Any other girl would have looked like she was wearing cardboard, but on screen I swear you would have thought Marilyn had on a pale, thin piece of silk. Her body was so fabulous it still came through".

Let's not forget the most visually stunning part of this iconic dress, the oversized butterfly bow at the back. The bow was boned and stuffed full of ostrich

LEFT A detail of the invisible wire used to hold the bow in place.

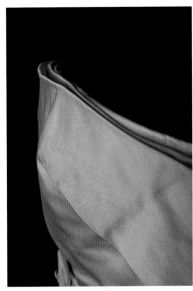

feathers and horsehair to maintain its shape and was held up by invisible thread attached to the belt.

The creation of the bodice is a more complicated story. Travilla hated flesh hanging over the top of a dress and any creasing in the stomach area and, of course, he could show no cleavage. To avoid all this he used inventive boning. The dress has three layers to the bodice, which gives a concertina effect to the bust line, but is, in fact, there for more practical reasons. The first layer is the boning which runs in a V-shape from the waist to the sides with one bone running straight up the middle. This held the breasts where they should be without pushing them up and kept the fabric flush to the body. The second and third layers were folded at the bust line, then attached at the waist, allowing the bodice to appear to move freely. The top layer was slightly less form-fitting, so stopped any creasing and gave an illusion of simplicity that was far from the truth – this dress was incredibly complicated. The bust line was also high at the front and low at the back to create a clean line that allowed no underarm flesh to escape, achieved by boning the first layer of fabric up the sides so that it was slightly higher than the other two layers, thus pushing back any unsightly bulging flesh.

Travilla was a unique designer who looked at everything he created from an architectural perspective as well as an aesthetic one. It is this that makes this dress a work of pure genius. Without the ingenious boning the incredibly heavy dress, with its high front and low back, would never have stayed up. According to Travilla, Marilyn never had to hitch her dress up at the bust, as you so often see actresses and celebrities doing nowadays – it stayed exactly where it should be, never moving.

The attention to detail was microscopic. Matching gloves were made in the same silk satin fabric, apart from the palms which were made from cotton, allowing Marilyn to grip when performing her dance routine. Beautiful hair and

ABOVE LEFT A detailed look at the three layers of fabric in the bodice plus the unusual dart.

ABOVE RIGHT Marilyn about to wiggle those famous hips of hers. This demonstrates perfectly the fluidity of movement the dress offered.

big jewellery finished the ensemble and, finally, the now famous "Diamonds Are a Girl's Best Friend" dress was created.

What is so remarkable is that, watching the film, you would swear that Marilyn was wearing a bias-cut soft silk satin dress because you can see the shape of her tummy and you can see her thighs. In fact, you can see clearly the shape of her body, despite Travilla's attempts to cover it up. But there was a quality that you could never hide in Marilyn; it couldn't be concealed even with a piece of fabric that was as heavy as leather. Fortunately Travilla also managed to fool the censors, letting us see Marilyn in all her fabulous glory!

OPPOSITE Diamonds definitely are a girl's best friend.

BELOW Two friends. Marilyn and Jane on setof Gentlemen Prefer Blondes, reading a song sheet.

"*Diamonds are a Girl's Best Friend*"

(song lyrics) Jule Styne

The Purple Dress

It is hard to be selective when it comes to Travilla's creations as they all are so beautiful. But in creating the stunning purple pleated gown for Marilyn Monroe to wear in the film *How to Marry a Millionaire* (1953), the costume designer reached a new high – as did the actress with her performance in the film.

The plot of *How to Marry a Millionaire* sees three New York models, Schatze, Pola and Loco, move into a Manhattan penthouse apartment and set out to find eligible millionaire bachelors to marry. Two of the women find potential candidates, but all three also fall in love with other men who are not as financially secure. Each woman now faces a dilemma: do they choose love or money?

The three female leads in the movie are played by Lauren Bacall, Betty Grable and Marilyn Monroe – a more glamorous cast is hard to imagine. After the success of her film *Gentleman Prefer Blondes* (1953), Marilyn had finally reached the ranks of bona fide movie star; her years of playing bit parts were over and she even had her own star on Hollywood Boulevard. *How to Marry a Millionaire* became the first comedy to be released in Cinemascope, the original "wide-screen" technique, that was technologically innovative at its time. The studio did have some concerns as to whether a comedy would work in the cinemascope format so, in order to maximize the chances of the film being a hit, they pulled together their enviable resources by featuring the top three blondes – and potentially the top three egos – under contract to Fox.

OPPOSITE Marilyn Monroe, Lauren Bacall and Betty Grable in the fashion show scene in How to Marry a Millionaire. The ribbon in Marilyn's shoes could be changed depending on what colour she was wearing.

BELOW Marilyn travelling on a plane in How to Marry a Millionaire. She is acting out that she cannot see without her glasses.

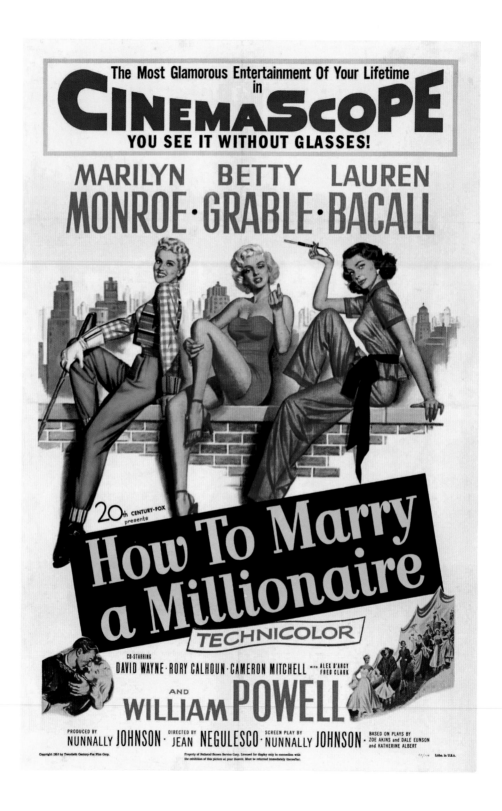

Just as the entertainment press had eagerly anticipated a feud between Marilyn Monroe and Jane Russell during the filming of *Gentlemen Prefer Blondes*, so too were they hoping for some sparks to fly between Marilyn and Betty Grable on the set of *Millionaire*. But Grable was incredibly kind to Marilyn, harbouring no resentment towards the newest blonde on the Fox lot. In fact, the older actress had defended Marilyn earlier that year over the controversy concerning the sensational gold lamé dress she wore to the *Photoplay* Awards, telling reporters that she was "a shot in the arm for Hollywood".

There were also no problems with the third actress, Lauren Bacall, who later wrote in her autobiography, *By Myself and Then Some* (2005): "A scene often went to 15 or more takes... not easy, often irritating. And yet I didn't dislike Marilyn. She had no meanness in her, no bitchery... There was something sad about her, wanting to reach out, afraid to trust, uncomfortable. She made no effort for others and yet she was nice."

During the making of *How to Marry a Millionaire* the Cinemascope filming technique presented a serious problem for Travilla. The new format required the use of a special anamorphic lens and wider screens. Despite the fact that it produced an intense and vibrant picture, from a costume designer's point of view the magnification of Cinemascope was a nightmare as it was so difficult to flatter the figures of the actresses in this new, artificially wide format.

ABOVE A costume test shot of Marilyn in *How to Marry a Millionaire*. This is one of the few of Marilyn's costumes for the movie that was not tight and figure-hugging.

LEFT Marilyn with Betty Grable. Marilyn is wearing a white version of the "Diamonds Are A Girl's Best Friend" dress made for her by Travilla for her personal use (see pages 148–149).

OPPOSITE The film poster for *How to Marry a Millionaire*.

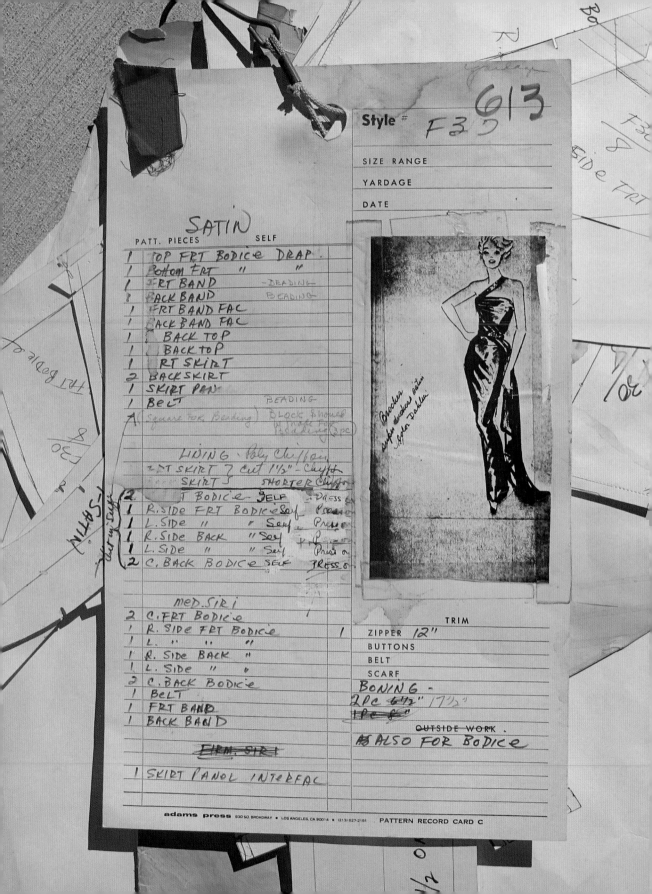

Style # F3 **613**

SIZE RANGE

YARDAGE

DATE

SATIN

PATT. PIECES		SELF
1	TOP FRT BODICE DRAP.	
1	BOTTOM FRT "	
1	FRT BAND	—BEADING—
8	BACK BAND	BEADING
1	FRT BAND FAC	
1	BACK BAND FAC	
1	BACK TOP	
1	BACK TOP	
1	FRT SKIRT	
2	BACK SKIRT	
1	SKIRT PAN.	
1	BELT	BEADING
A	(SQUARE FOR BEADING) BLOCK SHOULD W (MADE FOR BEADING (3 PC

LINING · Poly Chiffon
2 FRT SKIRT } cut 1½" — Chiffon
SKIRT } SHORTER Chiffon

2	FRT BODICE SELF	— DRESS E
1	R. SIDE FRT BODICE SELF	PRESS
1	L. SIDE " " SELF	PRESS
1	R. SIDE BACK " SELF	P
1	L. SIDE " " SELF	PRESS O
2	C. BACK BODICE SELF	PRESS O

MED. SIRI
2	C. FRT BODICE	
1	R. SIDE FRT BODICE	
1	L. " " "	
1	R. SIDE BACK "	
1	L. SIDE " "	
2	C. BACK BODICE	
1	BELT	
1	FRT BAND	
1	BACK BAND	

FIRM. SIRI

1 SKIRT PANEL INTERFAC

TRIM

1	ZIPPER 12"
	BUTTONS
	BELT
	SCARF
	BONING —
	2 PC 6½" 17½"
	1 PC 6"

OUTSIDE WORK

AS ALSO FOR BODICE

adams press 830 SO. BROADWAY • LOS ANGELES, CA 90014 • (213) 627-2181   PATTERN RECORD CARD C

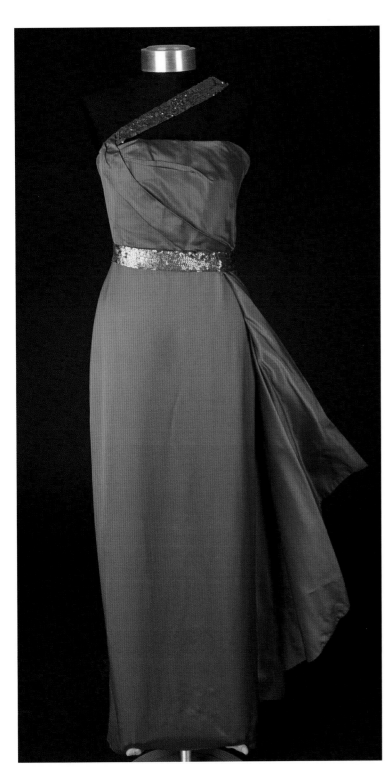

LEFT Travilla's prototype of the dahlia dress. You can see the extra fabric to the side. The extra train was attached from hidden hooks inside the sequin belt.

OPPOSITE The original pattern for the dahlia costume. Damaged from water, this has a photocopy in place of the original pencil sketch. It also looks like it has been played with over the years, hence the use of correcting fluid. There are many pieces to this pattern.

Travilla explained, "The heads of the studio and technical departments insisted that there were no distortions with 'scope'". But, in truth, the distortions were terrible, so bad that they could not shoot close-ups at all and everyone most definitely appeared wider." Travilla's female leads were unhappy with the landscape and magnified effect, especially as they were all asked to wear voluminous 1950s skirts. Bacall and Grable eventually relented but Marilyn did not – she demanded that she wore tight skirts throughout most of the movie and Travilla had to work with this.

The purple dress Travilla created for a particular scene from the movie has become another very famous image of Monroe. The scene sees the three girls all on different dates at the same venue. They all meet in the glamorous bathroom to exchange notes on their respective companions. All three are wearing totally different dresses that show off each of their figures perfectly. However, Marilyn steals the show, as she plays a girl who is hilariously nearsighted, but hates to wear her glasses when any man might see her. As she puts it, "Men aren't attentive to girls who wear glasses." As the other women leave, Marilyn is on her own, standing in front of a bank of four mirrors that shows her and the dress off beautifully.

OPPOSITE The costume test shot of the back view of the dahlia dress.

TOP LEFT AND ABOVE This shows the start of the unusual boning that travelled around the bust.

ABOVE LEFT A close-up of the belt from the side. You can see the pleating around the waist.

Created out of purple, or "dahlia" as Travilla called it, silk satin, there is a serious amount of construction to this dress. The bodice is extraordinary and almost architectural in a design that begins under the right arm. When you first look at it, the bodice appears to be straight across the bust line but it is not. In fact, it is considerably lower on the right side, which is where the sequin strap starts, and higher on the left side. This is because of the strap coming diagonally across the neckline. The dress gives the illusion of being straight across, but, if it had actually been cut straight across the bodice, the sequin detail would have made it appear lopsided.

There is, as always with Travilla, more unusual boning: on both sides a bone starts at the waistline directly above the hip and goes straight up to below the underarm, moulding to the body as it goes. Then, attached to the bottom of the first bone, another goes out to the centre of the each breast. Where the shoulder strap starts under the right arm the fabric is pleated, first with small pleats that travel horizontally across the bust line, then with larger pleats that are wrapped and sewn over the shoulder strap and under the arm, travelling diagonally around to the waist. These larger pleats are then attached to a separate train, also pleated, giving the illusion that the train starts by being attached to the shoulder strap and continues through in one complete length of fabric. A sequin belt is stitched on to hide the seam.

The Cinemascope technique attracted as much comment as the movie itself, and its stars came in for much scrutiny. But Marilyn Monroe was praised both

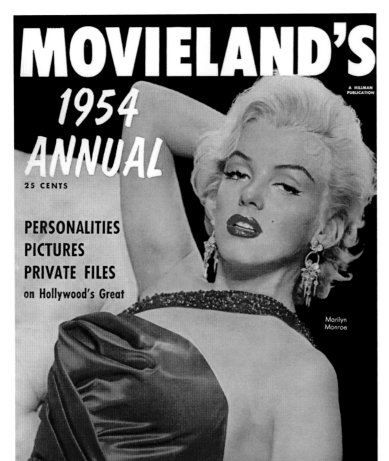

LEFT The front cover of a magazine dedicated to celebrity which featured Marilyn Monroe in the stunning purple dress.

OPPOSITE Marilyn in that famous mirror scene in *How to Marry a Millionaire*. This picture shows the fit and style of the dress from every angle.

for her appearance and her acting ability as illustrated in this quote from the *New York Herald Tribune* at the time: "The big question 'How does Marilyn Monroe look stretched across a broad screen?' is easily answered. If you insisted on sitting in the front row, you would probably feel as though you were being smothered in baked Alaska. Her stint as a deadpan comedienne is as nifty as her looks. Playing a near-sighted charmer who won't wear her glasses when men are around, she bumps into furniture and reads books upside down with a limpid guile that nearly melts the screen... *How To Marry A Millionaire* is measured, not in square feet, but in the size of the Johnson–Negulesco comic invention and the shape of Marilyn Monroe – and that is about as sizable and shapely as you can get."

Marilyn knew she had made it to the very top of her trade and was determined to shine at the movie's premiere. It took over six hours of hard work by William Travilla, Alan "Whitey" Snyder, Marilyn's make-up artist, and her hairdresser, Gladys Rasmussen, to prepare her for her entrance. She was sewn into a dress borrowed from the studio wardrobe: a flesh-coloured crepe-de-chine with shimmering sequins, accessorized with long white evening gloves and a white fox stole and muff. She had well and truly arrived

LEFT Marilyn at the premiere of *How to Marry a Millionaire*.

OPPOSITE A publicity shot of Marilyn and some lucky chap.

Tropical Heatwave

By promising Marilyn the lead role in the film version of the successful stage play *The Seven Year Itch*, 20th Century Fox persuaded Marilyn to appear in the star-studded musical *There's No Business Like Show Business* (1954), a tribute to Irving Berlin. This was the first movie Marilyn was to make after her marriage to Joe DiMaggio, who was so unimpressed by the actress's skimpy costumes that he refused to pose for pictures with her on his rare visits to the set.

The movie chronicles some 20 years in the lives of a showbiz family named the Donahues, the roles of the parents played by Dan Dailey and Ethel Merman. Two of the couple's three grown-up children, played by Donald O'Connor and Mitzi Gaynor, carry on the family tradition of show business, while a third, played by Johnny Ray, decides to become a priest. The Donald O'Connor character falls in love with a beautiful hat-check girl named Vicky, with ambitions of her own, played to perfection by Marilyn Monroe. He loses all sense of perspective while under her spell and, to escape his descent into alcoholism, joins the navy. After a search by his father he is finally reunited with his family and his lost love, Vicky, during a massive finale production number.

Its liveliest production number was a torrid version of "Heat Wave" performed by Marilyn and a bevy of male dancers, choreographed by Jack Cole. Needless to say, it was considered controversial for the time. The hip-wriggling and thrusting that were part of the choreography revealed the black leotard-bottom

PREVIOUS PAGE Travillia's sketch for the costume Marilyn wore for the "Heat Wave" number.

ABOVE Marilyn posing for a costume test shot in her "Heat Wave" costume.

OPPOSITE LEFT Marilyn performing the famous number in the film.

RIGHT The hat used in the dance routine.

FAR RIGHT The original costume on a mannequin.

BOTTOM RIGHT This image shows the inside detailing of the dress.

LEFT Marilyn performing the "Heat Wave" number in *There's No Business Like Show Business*.

LEFT One of the posters for *There's No Business Like Show Business* showing Marilyn wearing the dress she sand "Heat Wave" in.

underneath her costume, and many observers, unaccustomed to this sort of display, were outraged. Bosley Crowther of *The New York Times* stated that Marilyn's "wriggling and squirming… are embarrassing to behold." And *Time* magazine intoned that "Marilyn… bumps and grinds as expressively as the law will allow."

As costume designer, Travilla had plenty of censor issues too. The dress as shown in the sketch had nothing around Marilyn's midriff, however the censors insisted that Travilla add a piece of fabric to cover her belly button. Although the designer did as he was asked in the actual costume, he never did add that part to the sketch. Even with this addition, it is hard to believe that such a risqué dress made it past the censors – but it did and Travilla must have had tremendous fun creating such a flamboyant outfit.

It is easy to see where Travilla's inspiration came from for this raunchy design which is almost flamenco in style. He loved Spain and enjoyed watching the Spanish dancers on his many trips there. The design started with a hat, a close-fitting black turban with a huge, wide-brimmed plaited hat, which wasn't actually made of straw, but appeared to be. The ends of the straw were left raw to give the hat movement and, to add even more drama, huge silk flowers were attached to the hat. It was only after the hat was completed that Travilla took it to another level and added the flowers that hung around Marilyn's face.

The top of the outfit was essentially a sheath of black that was tied in the middle by a vivid pink and black chiffon scarf that crossed Marilyn's chest, draping down the back. Attached to the top were large black sequins that moved as she did.

The skirt started with an extremely tight band of fabric that gathered around her bottom at the back and pulled round to the front in a deep, revealing V-shape, with black sequins sewn to it; the undergarment was attached to this. From the front V, travelling round to below her bottom, was a voluminous skirt of hand-printed white fabric with huge black flowers. Attached to these flowers were hundreds of large sequins scattered and sewn randomly. The interior of the skirt is the same fabric as the scarf – a plain pink chiffon, gathered and attached in many layers travelling from top to bottom. These layers also had hundreds of scattered sequins, this time transparent ones.

Sadly the film was not a success either critically or commercially, but it did enable Marilyn to take on what was to become arguably her most successful role – the Girl in *The Seven Year Itch*.

Travilla

The White Dress

Travilla might have dismissed the stunning dress he designed for Marilyn Monroe to wear in the famous subway scene from the movie *The Seven Year Itch* (1955) as "that silly little dress", but to many it is the most famous dress in cinema history. It is one of those images that has permanently lodged itself in the world's subconscious, re-awakened at the oddest moments, and it is so iconic that there is virtually no one who has not seen it. But why has this particular image has become so legendary? Is it the fact that Marilyn is showing a lot of flesh, so scandalous in the 1950s, or simply because of who she is and the drama that surrounded her life? Whatever the combination of factors that propelled this image to stardom, the one thing that has been overlooked is the dress itself.

Many people have viewed and marvelled at this glamorous dress, wanted a copy for themselves or worn a poor imitation at a fancy dress party but the real story behind it, both in the dress's inception and in achieving that memorable shot of Marilyn wearing it, is far more complicated.

For a start the original filmed sequence, where the dress blows up around Marilyn's wide-planted legs as she stands over a subway grating, never made it to the screen. The footage was shot on Manhattan's Lexington Avenue at 52nd Street on

ABOVE LEFT Marilyn sits in the famous white dress during a break from filming *The Seven Year Itch* with director Billy Wilder.

OPPOSITE The crew take an interest during the filming of one of the most famous scenes in Hollywood history.

110

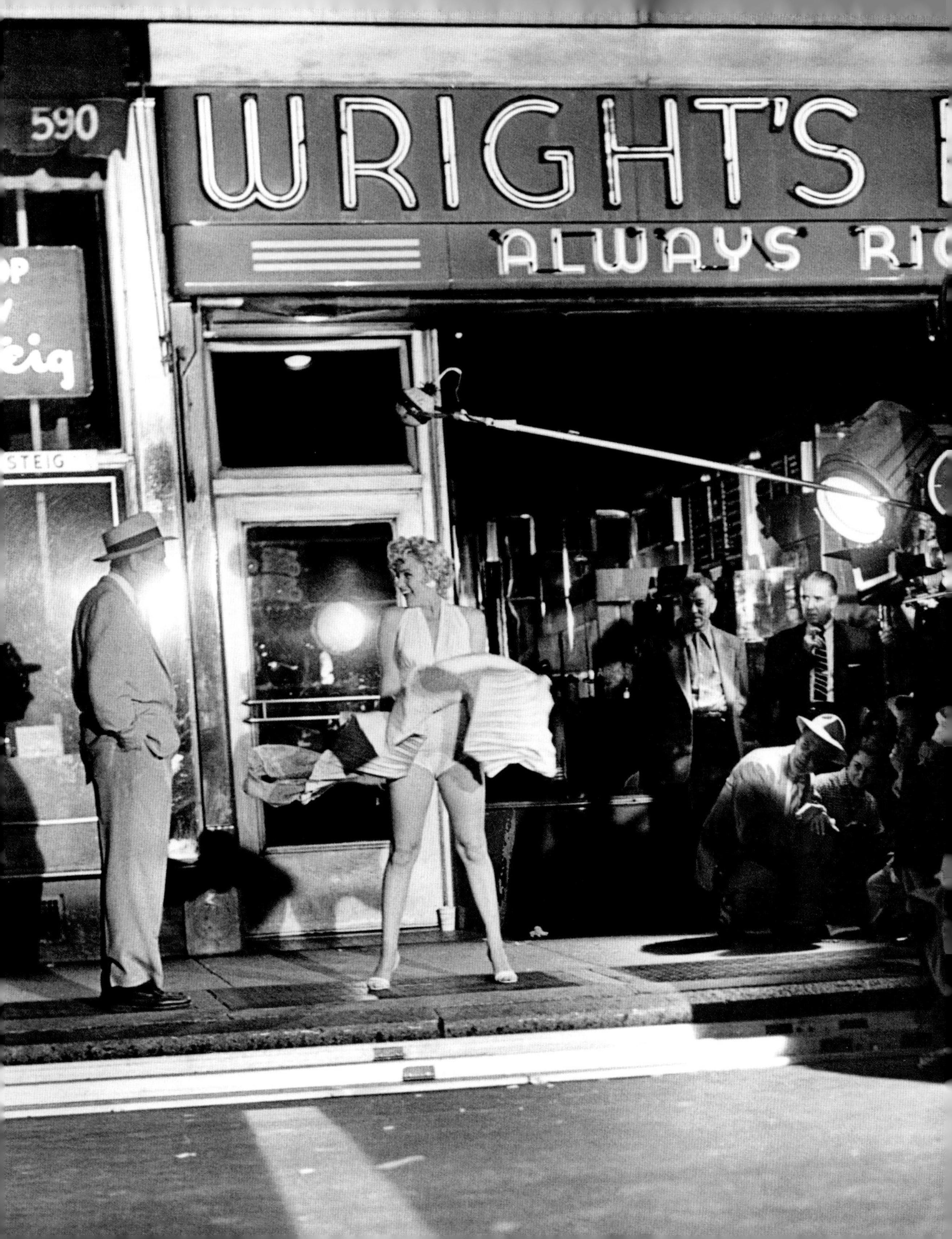
590
WRIGHT'S
ALWAYS
STEIG

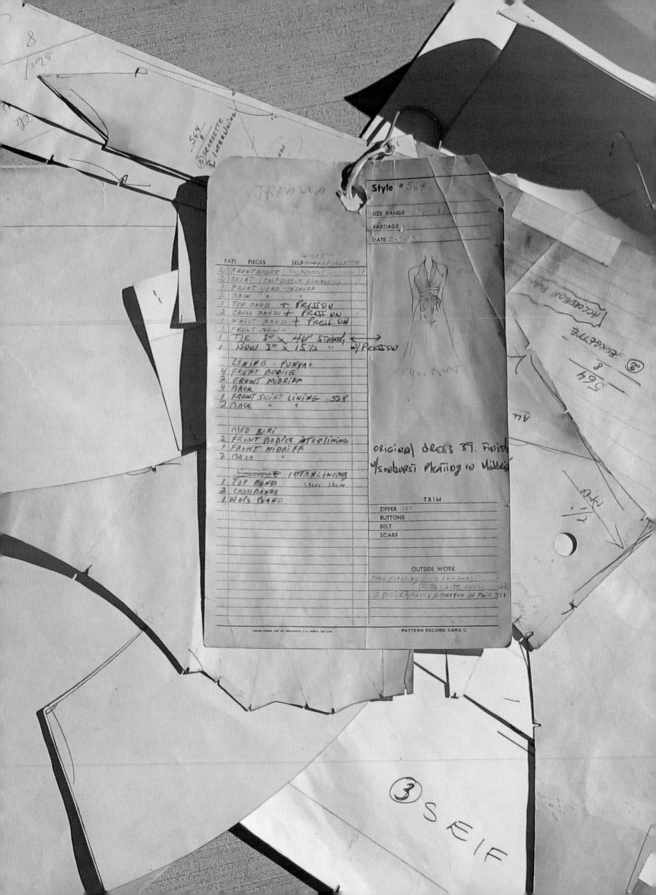

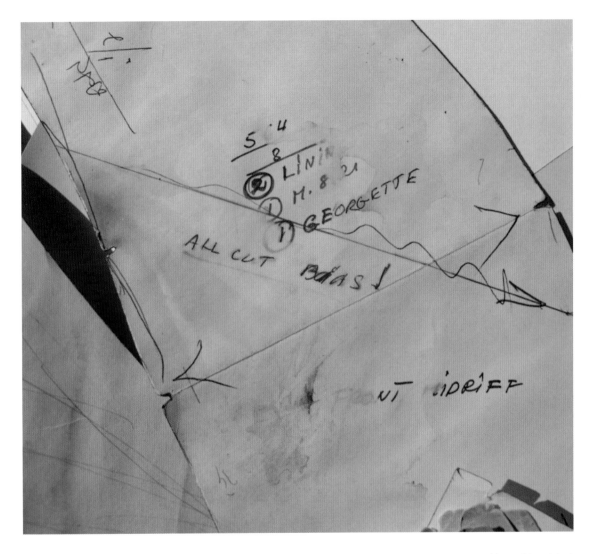

15 September 1955 at 1.00am. Five thousand onlookers whistled and cheered
through take after take as Marilyn repeatedly fluffed her lines. Witnessing the scene
was an increasingly embarrassed and angry Joe DiMaggio, Monroe's husband at the
time. Some believe that this night was the start of their marriage breakdown and that
dress and that image proved to be too much for a man who wanted his wife to cover
up, not show off. The noise of the crowd made these first takes unusable. Director
Billy Wilder subsequently restaged the scene on the 20th Century Fox lot and got a
more satisfactory result.

One witness to the public shots was the Italian actress Gina Lollobrigida,
who happened to be filming in New York at the time. As Lollobrigida described in
an interview with Henry-Jean Servat for *Paris Match*, published in August 2002, "I
learnt that Marilyn was doing the outdoor scenes of *Seven Year Itch* a few blocks
away. Rupert Allen [their mutual press officer] had the idea of organizing a meeting. I

learned later that she was not too sure about it as she did not like confrontation. She was frightened by the idea of being face to face with such a star. I do not feel that fear, both because I am very sure of myself and because I felt a secret affection for her. I found her very beautiful and very talented, I was not jealous. She was a dazzling sun….

"We went by limo and turned the corner into Lexington Avenue and 52nd Street. People were everywhere so they ushered me to the front where I stood and watched that famous scene. Marilyn seemed to radiate and had a lot of fun filming this sequence under the gaze of thousands of people who idolized her. After filming, Rupert Allen led me to Marilyn, who was still wearing the white pleated dress that has now been rendered immortal. By curious chance I myself was wearing a white dress very similar to hers. She gave me her hand, she smiled from the heart and I returned the favour. We stayed for a long time talking about movies, Hollywood and our dresses. Immediately we felt like two women, not two competing stars.

LEFT Another shot of that famous scene. How she didn't fall through the grate in those heals is a mystery!

"It amazed me because she had no arrogance. She seemed shy in the extreme and spoke in a small voice, muffled and barely perceptible. She made no attempt at all to dazzle or overpower me. When a photographer from Fox tried to take a picture of the two of us, she nodded but begged him to make sure it was ok. We then hugged and promised to meet up with each other very soon."

Another witness to the original scene, standing apart from the crowds with a pained look on his face, was Travilla. As he turned to leave he was stopped by one of the film crew's young attendants. "Mr Travilla?" she called and as he turned towards her she handed him a pen and a copy of a script entitled *The Seven Year Itch*. "Could you autograph this for me?" she asked, "…and maybe put a note on there asking Marilyn too? She'll do it for you." Such was the influence Travilla had over the famous actress.

The design that Travilla created for the dress was far quicker than the filming of the scene; he was so inspired that he produced the entire costume ensemble for *The Seven Year Itch* out over one weekend. When asked to create the costumes for

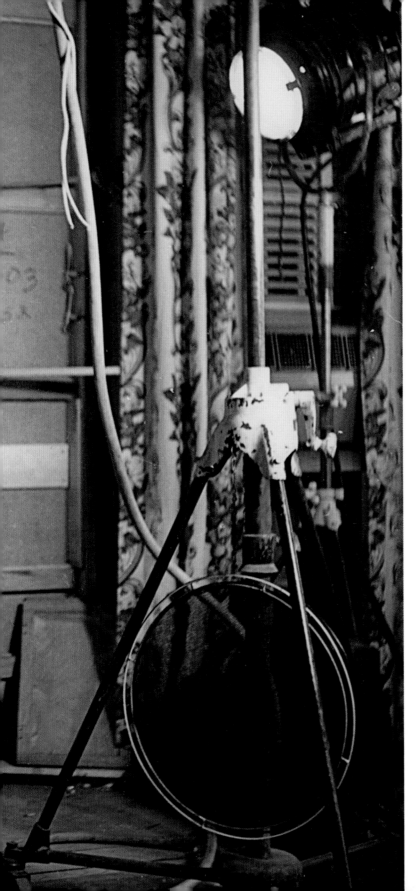

LEFT A stunning image of Marilyn in
another of the costumes from *The Seven
Year Itch*. She is seen here walking off the
set offering an opportunity to see one of
Travilla's designs from the back.

" *That silly little dress* "

–William Travilla

LEFT A close-up of the bodice showing the bow clearly tying to the left, not the front as for many copies. The belt was originally stitched to the dress across the back to the hips then free to be hand-tied. Over the years the belt has come away. Rather than replacing it as it once was it has been tied into a bow and stitched to the waist as one piece, as seen here. You can also see here that the pleats around the bodice are actually stitched into place

OPPOSITE Lights, camera, action! Press shots for that famous image.

this movie Travilla had been delighted on many levels. First, there was the obvious pleasure in working with Marilyn but, as important, was that the movie was shot in New York. Travilla loved New York and spent a lot of time there and he knew just how to evoke the feeling of the Big Apple.

After his frenzied weekend of designing Travilla showed Marilyn his ideas and, as she always did, she approved them all. The role she was to play was simply "The Girl"; sensuous and beautiful, her character still had to possess a sweet and innocent demeanour. So Travilla had to portray Marilyn as pure and lovely, almost talcum-powder clean. Achieving this effect on a humid, sunny afternoon in New York was not an easy task.

The script presented challenges too. Travilla knew the halter-neck dress with its sunburst pleats would have to blow up at some point in the movie. So the fabric he chose was an ivory coloured rayon-acetate crepe, heavy enough to flow beautifully as she walked but still light enough to blow up in an interesting way. It is clear just by looking at the pictures that the dress did not blow up vertically like so many of the copies have done; instead it billowed, allowing her to pose seductively among the pleats of the skirt. Travilla never normally used manmade fabric, but with pleating this posed a challenge, as 100 per cent natural fabric would not hold such stiff pleats so, for all his pleated creations, a special fabric with just a small amount of manmade fibre in it to maintain the structure had to be made.

And there was one other problem, characteristic of Marilyn. The fact that the actress never wore underwear and point-blank refused to wear any until the scene was shot, had to be taken into consideration. According to Travilla, "she hated wearing underclothes... but if you are that perfect why spoil the line?"

The Seven Year Itch dress was boned, not in pliable polyester as it might be today, but in metal. As a result the halter neck lay flat against Marilyn's chest and the bodice was moulded exactly to the contours of her body. This allowed her to move totally freely without the worry of anything falling out. The attention to detail did not stop there: each pleat was hand-formed then sewn into place. The original pattern clearly shows the number of pieces that make up this dress.

Bill Sarris recalls: "In those days you were not allowed to show cleavage, but Bill always talked about how, because of how Marilyn's breast were, you could cut a dress fairly low and still not show breast. Sarris also revealed another trick Travilla employed: he would take a little half-ball button and sew it inside the costume where the nipple would be so that Marilyn's nipples always appeared pert. According to Sarris, Travilla "had all kinds of tricks up his sleeve. When he worked up the sketch for the skirt-blowing scene I'm sure he didn't think it was going to become the most famous dress in the world."

In the 1977 book *Hollywood Costume*, Dale McConathy and legendary *Vogue* editor Diana Vreeland accused Travilla of buying the dress off the rack. Naturally Travilla was furious and mystified as to why they would write something like that; furthermore he asserted that in the studio era everything was designed especially for the screen. As anyone who has seen the original will testify, there is nothing "off the rack" about it. The book haunted Travilla for years but vindication came later in his life as, using his "original" patterns, he made two identical copies of the dress; one is still in the estate and another was bought a few years ago by a private collector for a large amount of money. Travilla also used this dress as the

ABOVE A rare picture showing Marilyn with a scarf in hand which seems to disappear in later pictures.

OPPOSITE The famous billboard of Marilyn in Times Square for the release of the movie.

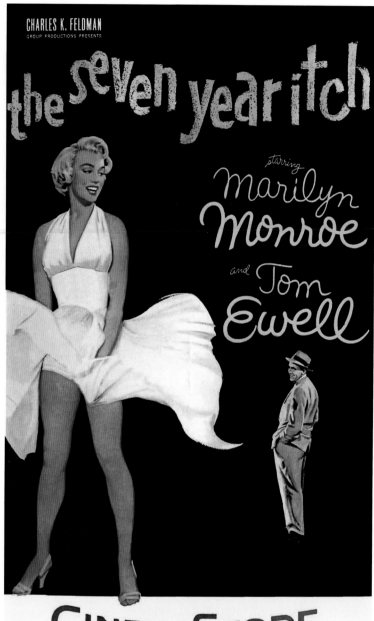

opening to his catwalk fashion shows. He would always use a brunette or black model, in striking contrast to Marilyn's bleached blondeness, and send her down the catwalk saying "…now here is a dress you all might recognize".

In the early 1980s Travilla travelled to London to promote his work in the Littlewoods catalogue, which was widely known in the UK at the time. A copy of the dress from *The Seven Year Itch* was on display, along with millions of pounds worth of jewellery. There was a break-in after the show and the only thing stolen was the dress, but whoever stole it obviously panicked at its fame and returned it via a newspaper the following day.

What has always fascinated me about this dress is that all the copies I have seen have always had the bow placed at the front. In reality, it was a self-tied bow, tied to the left and hung down the hip. So, despite the numerous photos of this dress, that one thing seems to have been overlooked.

Another thing I always hear is that the dress is white. When I point out that actually it is bone coloured people look at me disbelievingly. The explanation lies

in the advances in filming during this period which gave a whole new meaning to "complicated" as far as costume designers were concerned. On colour film designers would have to work with the colour spectrum as it appeared on celluloid, not as it really was. A beautiful blue may appear grey on film, requiring a screen test for every garment. The white dress for *The Seven Year Itch* was cream, or bone, as Travilla called it. White would have looked grey and murky on film but cream looked white. The same problems arose with the costume he created for the *"Diamonds Are a Girl's Best Friend"* extravaganza.

Other costumes for *The Seven Year Itch* included some very tight numbers. Marilyn insisted that all her costumes be skin-tight. Travilla noted in an interview for the *LA Times* in September 1980, "We argued about her costumes for *The Seven Year Itch* many times, but she never gave in. When she wore them she had a certain innocence that kept her from seeming vulgar. Many of those dresses were so tight she had to be sewn into them every morning. If she gained a pound or two they would not fit."

ABOVE A costume test shot of another of the costumes from *The Seven Year Itch*. This was, again, a costume Marilyn was sewn into.

OPPOSITE A screen shot of both stars – Marilyn Monroe and Tom Ewell.

THIS PAGE Another stunning publicity shot of Marilyn for *The Seven Year Itch*, this time wearing a tiger pattern dress with black tulle.

Travilla

The Stripper

One of several roles Marilyn was being considered for in late 1962 was Lila, a small-town stripper with Hollywood dreams and aspirations, for a film to be entitled *The Stripper* (1963). It was based on the 1959 stage play *A Loss of Roses* by William Inge, who also wrote *Bus Stop* (1956), another Monroe vehicle. The costumes for the movie were to be designed by Travilla. In the event, however, after Marilyn's untimely death in 1962, Joanne Woodward took over the role.

Travilla had not designed for Marilyn since 1954 and recalled that, "I was really looking forward to working with her again." Sadly, their working reunion never happened so the costume sketches Travilla had made with Marilyn in mind were put away in the estate archives, where they remained for more than 45 years away from the public eye, until their recent discovery in preparation for this book. There was a huge level of excitement when they were found. The sketches of other Marilyn dresses have been seen for many years but it had been assumed that, as Marilyn had passed away before production, nothing would have been saved from Travilla's original work with her on this film.

Travilla – unusually for a costume designer – drew illustrations clearly depicting the actress who was to wear the outfit he was designing, which in many cases meant Marilyn. The illustrations for this movie show a more mature and refined Marilyn than in their earlier collaborations, though the smaller image in the top right corner of the risqué black sketch (*see* page 128) is clearly an "homage" to his iconic white dress design from *The Seven Year Itch* (1955). Travilla must have drawn it to amuse Marilyn, as the dress is blowing up and her hand is covering her modesty.

Marilyn would have played this part very differently and her costumes were far more revealing than those later designed for Joanne Woodward. But Joanne put in a fabulous performance and made the character her own. Both Bill Sarris and Travilla adored Woodward. Travilla designed for her in films including *Sign Post to Murder* (1964) and *From the Terrace* (1960). Sarris recalls a story that shows their closeness and also Joanne's humour. "Every year Bill and I would hold an event at the Greek Church in Los Angeles. We would raise money for charity, but it was really a great way to get people together and have lots of fun. Joanne Woodward was a brilliant stage performer, very funny with a fabulous voice. We asked her on a couple of occasions if she would perform at the event… she of course said yes. At one particular event she was due to attend, she called Travilla saying that she was really sick and was so sorry but she just could not make it. He was concerned for her and told her not to worry. Joanne said that she was sending someone else in her place. She would not tell him who it was. Then, just before the show was about to start, who should show up but her husband, Paul Newman. Paul was a fabulous actor and lovely man but he was not used to the stage. Bless him, you could tell he was very uncomfortable. Everyone in the audience was agog… [They] just wanted to look at him, being the most handsome and charismatic man that he was. He was so sweet to have done it for us but I know Joanne made him do it."

Travilla's working relationship with Joanne Woodward was a resounding success and the designer received his fourth and final Academy Award nomination for the movie. In a brilliant coup, the original "stripper", Gypsy Rose Lee, starred in this movie as Madam Olga.

PAGE 128 Sketches for *The Stripper* costumes. The main image shows a two-piece, black-sequined outfit with a bright purple flower adornment.

OPPOSITE A rather more demure white dress. The design features a diagonal strip that uses a special technique which creates small uniform holes in the fabric.

PAGE 132 Travilla's sketch for Marilyn's costume in *The Stripper*. As one can see from the sketch, it would have been a risqué costume with its detachable skirt.

PAGE 133 Further sketches of costumes for *The Stripper*. The butterfly detail on the leg is incredibly unique.

Travilla

Personal Dresses

These gowns were for a friend not for any movie. "

William Travilla

During their relationship Travilla designed many of Marilyn's personal dresses. Ocasionally over the years Travilla would take Marilyn's personal dresses out to look at them and remember the lovely woman who once wore them. Being for the star's personal use rather than for a movie role, the the way Travilla approached designing them changed entirely.

Bill Sarris explains that if the dress were to be worn for a party or for dinner with friends, then"It wasn't about press or pictures of her wearing them". According to Sarris, if Marilyn were around the studio or Travilla's house she would "often ask to borrow something and she always gave them back, which we never expected". Other personal gowns had to be more high profile. Sarris remembers that "The more dramatic personal gowns were made as part of the movie process so had to work with the film; we created these for events like premieres and award ceremonies. They were made for impact, to photograph beautifully. Very different."

These dresses have been kept away from the public eye for years. Sarris says that, "Travilla kept them because they meant so much to him. They were made for a friend and not for any movie, he only ever told a few people he had them and I have kept them for the same reasons."

When I visited Bill Sarris I felt honoured to hear him talk about these dresses as he never really has done before, again because of the constant attention he received from people when it came to Marilyn. He always emphasizes their friendship, not her fame, saying, "She was my friend first; I never got caught up in the actress part of her."

It is wonderful to have dresses that were so personal to Travilla and Bill Sarris still in the estate. There are few photographs or press cuttings showing Marilyn wearing them, but, as both men said, these were for a friend, so none of that matters. Travilla knew and that is all that counts.

The Pink Chiffon Dress

The pink chiffon gown is a prototype of the dress Marilyn wore in *Gentlemen Prefer Blondes*. In the movie Marilyn wore the dress when she and Jane Russell enter the ship's ballroom for dinner. It is a beautiful moment in the movie and Marilyn looks jaw-droppingly lovely in the dress, which was orange and covered in beads

OPPOSITE This sketch for the orange and pink dresses was the starting point. All that is missing is the beading.

and crystals. This pink version is almost identical apart from the shoulder strap which was changed slightly for the movie version. Both dresses exhibit Travilla's trademark flamboyance combined with attention to detail. Looking at the pattern, you can see a swatch of the original fabric attached and the fact sheet tells in minute detail where the beads and crystals are to be attached, for example: "straight for rhinestones".

The pink chiffon photographs beautifully. In reality, it is a salmon pink but, when it is shot on camera, the colour becomes very vivid. The dress for the movie was orange or "pumpkin", as Travilla called it. The similarity between the two is in the construction. Both are in the same chiffon fabric, with boning over the hip and waist that finishes under the arm. There is no boning in the bust area at all; the side boning keeps the shape perfectly and it almost stands on its own.

What is confusing to people who look at this dress is how Marilyn managed to get it on as there appears to be no zip. In fact, the zip is very cleverly hidden – amazingly, it is in the front of the dress.

OPPOSITE The original pattern for the dress. The original pink fabric is attached, however the orange fabric is identical.

BELOW LEFT Jane Russell and Marilyn Monroe's ballroom entrance in *Gentleman Prefer Blondes*.

BELOW RIGHT The pink chiffon dress with ruffles down the front and a matching stole.

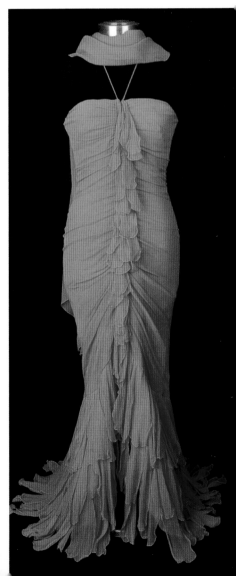

The Silver Dress

This beautiful silver lamé dress was originally designed for *Gentlemen Prefer Blondes* (1953). Ultimately, scenes of Marilyn wearing this gown were cut from the final film, however, Marilyn wore it to multiple public appearances, including the *Los Angeles Herald Examiner* Charity Event, held at the Shrine Auditorium on 4 December 1953. Marilyn also wore this dress to a very significant event in her life – to accept her *Photoplay* Award in 1954. The previous year, to the same awards ceremony, she had worn the very similar gold lamé gown which had caused such controversy. Like the gold gown, this silver one is sunburst-pleated and wraparound in style, with a jewel at the hip. It also has built-in underwear. (Courtesy of Greg Schreiner.)

ABOVE LEFT This shows the built-in underwear concealed in the dress.

BELOW LEFT A close-up view of the zip area of the dress. The internal lining and underwear were fixed in place with a multitude of hooks and eyes before the dress was zipped up.

RIGHT Travilla's sketch of the silver dress.

OPPOSITE The front and back view of this stunning sunburst silver lamé pleated gown.

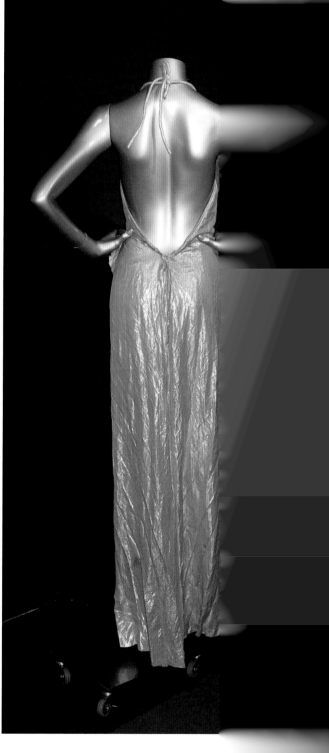

TOP LEFT A close-up view of the silver lamé dress. This is the original brooch sewn into place.

TOP RIGHT A detailed view of the hem of the silver dress.

RIGHT Marilyn prepping for an appearance, wearing this famous and beautiful dress.

OPPOSITE Marilyn dressed and ready to go, wearing her own fur with the silver lamé dress.

The Embroidered Dress

After six hours of preparation at Fox from William Travilla and her hairdresser and make-up artist, Marilyn arrived for the premiere of *How to Marry a Millionaire* in November 1953 wearing this dress borrowed from the studio and her own white Arctic fox stole. The dress is made up of a very sheer underdress with an overlay of hand-embroidered lace with hundreds of tiny hand-sewn crystals. The pleated satin train wraps from the right across the bust to the floor and the whole effect is truly stunning. Notice the change in the sash from satin to tulle in the photographs.

ABOVE A pulicity shot for *Gentlemen Prefer Blondes*, showing Marilyn lying on one of the deckchairs featured in the film.

LEFT Marilyn relaxes during the publicity shoot for *Gentlemen Prefer Blondes*.

OPPOSITE Marilyn's entrance for the prèmière of *Gentlemen Prefer Blondes*.

TOP A detailed look at the interior of the bodice. The metal boning is encased in the "V" piece of fabric.

ABOVE A close-up of the front of this dress which shows the seed pearls and bugle beads.

LEFT A full length shot of the stunning personal gown worn by Marilyn.

The Cream Dress

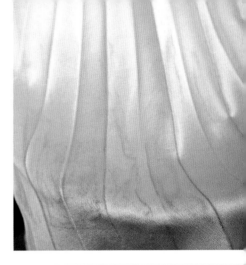

The cream dress is a beautiful – and very recognizable – design. It has a similar structure to, and is clearly based on, the infamous gold lamé gown that Marilyn Monroe wore in *Gentleman Prefer Blondes* (1953).

Made out of silk crepe, this cream dress, again, is hand-pleated and made out of one circle of fabric. The pleats are perfect, meeting exactly along the back seam. The neckline is boned in Travilla's famous V-shape and is covered in hand-sewn seed pearls on the bodice.

Bill remembers this dress vividly: "She borrowed it from us for an event that I cannot remember now, but when she brought it back there was a stain on the bottom. She apologized and said that it was raining that night and she had brushed up against the car when she got out of it and it left a dirty mark. She was very apologetic but it did not matter. It was Marilyn, you could forgive her anything." There is also another stain, a lipstick mark, on the bottom middle edge of the dress.

I did ask why it was never cleaned and Bill replied that he had no idea, "but there were so many dresses in the studio packed away in bags that it must have just been forgotten".

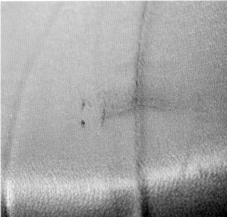

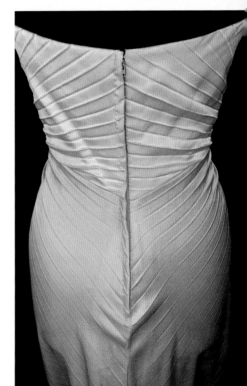

TOP Here you can see the stain on the hem of the dress.

MIDDLE The lipstick stain on the middle of the hem.

RIGHT The back of the dress and the remarkably even pleating. Each one matches perfectly.

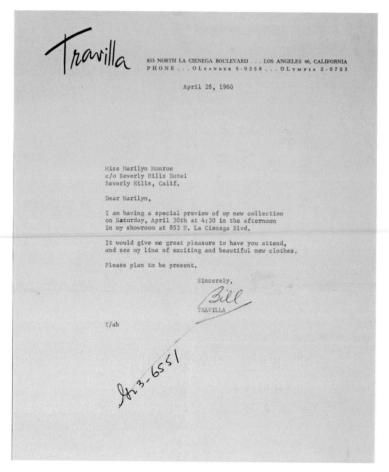

LEFT A letter Travilla sent to Marilyn inviting her to a preview for one of his collections in April 1960.

OPPOSITE Marilyn in the white version of the "Diamonds Are a girl's best friend" dress.

The White Dress

This is a rare colour shot of Marilyn wearing a white version of the "Diamonds Are a Girl's Best Friend" dress (minus the bow) at columnist Walter Winchell's birthday party held at Ciro's nightclub in April 1953. Following the death of his close friend Damon Runyan from cancer in 1946, Winchell established the Damon Runyan Cancer Reseach Foundation with the support of celebrities including Marilyn and Joe DiMaggio, Marlene Dietrich and Bob Hope.

Made in the same silk satin, with matching gloves, this gown is almost identical to the pink "Diamonds" dress. It has a slight train, unlike the pink version, and a detachable bow, with clever hidden poppers to attach it under a flap of fabric at the back.

Further Classics

Bus Stop

It is often stated that *Bus Stop* (1956) was Marilyn's favourite performance. She thought she did her best work in the film and it legitimized her as a serious actress. Marilyn plays Cherie, a saloon singer who hails from the Ozarks but is working her way across the Southwest towards Hollywood, where she hopes to be discovered and "get treated with a little respect, too". Bo, played by Don Murray, is a naive but stubborn cowboy who falls in love with the singer and tries to take her away on a bus, against her will, to get married and live on his ranch in Montana. He is finally stopped and is full of contrition, so Cherie forgives him and goes with him anyway.

One of the costumes Travilla designed for Marilyn was a blouse of pale green with a lace overlay. The hem at the bottom has an unfinished, raw edge to bolster the illusion that it is the kind of inexpensive garment, not properly finished, that Cherie would wear. It has a co-ordinating silk cord along the neckline and sleeves that is tied into a bow at the front. This is exactly the same blouse – though perhaps altered to fit Marilyn – that Susan Hayward had worn in *With a Song in My Heart* in 1952. This style of blouse, often referred to as "gypsy style", has been fashionable at many points since.

Marilyn liked her costumes for this movie, apart from the fishnet stockings. These Marilyn thought too perfect so she had them ripped and then deliberately poorly repaired, as she felt Cherie would not have had money to spare for new fishnet stockings, nor would they have been readily available in the small town she was in. Marilyn also went through the wardrobe with photographer and close friend Milton Greene to select pieces that would aptly express the character of Cherie.

When Marilyn sings "That Old Black Magic" she is wearing a green costume made of satin overlayed with sequins and gold tassels. Travilla purposely created this to look worn, to reflect Marilyn's character in the movie. He removed a few sequins here and there and lost part of the strap on one side. The chest area is a nude fabric overlayed with black net, which cleverly achieves the look of the corset having discoloured with age and it fits with the character Marilyn played perfectly.

ABOVE The green lace blouse worn by Marilyn in *Bus Stop*.

OPPOSITE The green showgirl costume from *Bus Stop*.

Don't Bother to Knock

This 1952 thriller, set in a New York hotel, proved that Marilyn Monroe, in a rare dramatic role, could most certainly act. She plays shy but psychotic Nell Forbes, who is babysitting for a wealthy couple dining in the hotel. Also staying there is pilot Jed Towers (Richard Widmark), who has just been jilted by his girlfriend, played by Anne Bancroft, a singer in the hotel bar. Jed ends up in the arms of Nell and discovers that she is dangerously unstable.

Marilyn's costumes in this movie were very understated, unlike many of her other films where sex appeal and glamour were the order of the day. These costumes help to show her shy character as, once again, costume and onscreen persona went faultlessly hand in hand.

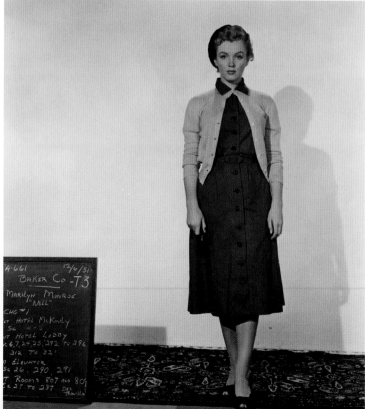

ABOVE Marilyn wore this very sexy chiffon negligee for the costume test for the scene in which Nell dresses up in clothes belonging to a hotel guest in order to seduce Richard Widmark's character, Jed. This is Marilyn at her best.

LEFT Marilyn's costume test for her first appearance as Nell, the troubled babysitter. This very simple, very "un-Marilyn", outfit shows perfectly the role she is to play in this film.

OPPOSITE Nell (Marilyn Monroe) and Lyn (Anne Bancroft) get into a tussle over Jed (Richard Widmark).

Gentlemen Prefer Blondes

The scene where Marilyn Monroe measures her bottom to see if she can fit through a porthole is a joy to watch. However, how she managed to get into that porthole in this very tight dress is a mystery. It is a stunning deep purple which appears to be black in the movie. Beautifully constructed and very unusual, the crepe dress has hand-sewn satin ribbon covering it. The satin train is one continuous piece of fabric; starting on one side, it wraps across the bust and goes down the other side.

BELOW LEFT AND CENTRE The stunning purple gown worn by Marilyn in *Gentlemen Prefer Blondes*. The dress is never seen without the jacket in the movie.

BELOW RIGHT Travilla's sketch for the purple dress.

In *Gentleman Prefer Blondes* (1953) Marilyn picks up the incriminating photographs wearing a black and brown check wool dress. In this shot, taken in Korea in 1954, she is wearing the same dress.

She and Joe DiMaggio were newlyweds on a trip in Japan, when Marilyn took a detour to Korea to entertain the troops. She performed ten shows in four days, in front of audiences that totalled more than 100,000 soldiers and marines. Later Monroe recalled that the trip "was the best thing that ever happened to me. I never felt like a star before in my heart. It was so wonderful to look down and see a fellow smiling at me."

ABOVE Marilyn entertaining the troops in Korea, 1954.

This beautiful black crepe dress is very closely fitted. A stole and muff adorn it to perfection and, when the stole is removed, there is a strategically placed gold necklace that twists through the fabric of the neckline.

ABOVE "Look round windows!": Marilyn on the set of *Gentlemen Prefer Blondes*.

LEFT Marilyn in a costume test shot for *Gentlemen Prefer Blondes*.

This white silk nightgown was created for *Gentlemen Prefer Blondes* but never made it into the movie. It was replaced by a towelling robe that was felt to work better in the context of the movie.

LEFT A costume test shot for *Gentlemen Prefer Blondes*. The silk nightgown was not actually used in the film.

In the original theatrical trailer of *Gentlemen Prefer Blondes*, Jane Russell and Marilyn Monroe were shown among dancers, climbing the steps of a slide in a children's playground, and singing "When the Wild Women Go Swimmin' Down in Bimini Bay" and "The Four French Dances". Even though this scene was cut, it makes an appearance on many of the movie posters and DVD covers. The costume Marilyn wore for the scene is rather risqué with the eye being drawn to the bow that is positioned directly above the crotch area. In yet another example of Travilla's genius for design and detail, it also has two rows of diamonds and tear drops on the thigh line, again to draw the eye strategically. Stunning handmade silk flowers adorn the neckline and the whole bodice is covered in sequins. This costume is now in the collection of David Gainsborough Roberts.)

ABOVE The back view of this risqué costume.

OPPOSITE LEFT An original costume from *Gentlemen Prefer Blondes*.

OPPOSITE RIGHT The original sketch of Jane Russell in the same costume as Marilyn is shown in.

LEFT Marilyn in a costume test shot for *Gentlemen Prefer Blondes* wearing a Napoleon style hat.

Travilla

This green one-piece with trousers and satin belt is a brave colour combination that works to great effect. It is worn when Marilyn discovers she has been caught in an innocent, yet rather incriminating, position in the scene where Piggy, the owner of a huge diamond mine, is explaining how a python, using himself as the python to demonstrate, can wrap itself around a goat – Marilyn, in this case, taking the part of the goat.

LEFT A promotional shot of Marilyn for *Gentlemen Prefer Blondes*.

For the double wedding on board the ship at the end of *Gentlemen Prefer Blondes* Jane and Marilyn wear identical dresses. As with the red dresses designed for the opening "Two Little Girls From Little Rock" number, Travilla had to create something that would suit them both. The design, which uses a full skirt, nipped-in waist and high neck, would enhance most women's figures and flattered both actresses beautifully. The dresses were made from white hand-embroidered lace over a chiffon full skirt. The skirt is shorter at the front than the back, which gives a lovely silhouette.

ABOVE Marilyn and Jane in the wedding scene in *Gentlemen Prefer Blondes*.

ABOVE LEFT This costume test shot shows Marilyn wearing the dress for wedding in the film.

163

Wearing this outfit when she is kicked out of the hotel in Paris, Marilyn, together with Jane Russell, sings "When Love Goes Wrong Nothing Goes Right". The beret seems appropriate as they are, after all, in Paris.

How to Marry a Millionaire

Made for *How to Marry a Millionaire*, this dress was never used in the film but Marilyn wore it for publicity purposes for the movie. Marilyn did on many occasions wear dresses cut from movies to premieres and publicity events. Travilla always liked his stars to wear a dress from the particular movie to such events as it gave the public a taste of what was to come in the film.

This very flattering dress has simple lines and is fitted over the hips with triangular panels from the knee down. Hand-sewn ribbon is around the waist and under the bust; this runs around the back and over the shoulder to create the straps. (Copyright of *Colección Maite Minguez Ricart*, www. colecciónmaiteminguez.com).

ABOVE This close-up view of the bodice and waist of this dress shows the detail of the hand-stitched ribbon.

LEFT Marilyn's gown used in publicity shots for *How to Marry a Millionaire*.

Monkey Business

This rollicking 1952 comedy featured Cary Grant, Marilyn Monroe, Ginger Rogers and a mischievous chimpanzee. Cary Grant plays a research chemist trying to invent a youth potion, Ginger Rogers is his wife and Marilyn Monroe is his boss's secretary.

ABOVE The back shot of one-piece swimsuit.

LEFT Marilyn's costume test for her pool scene with Cary Grant, wearing Travilla's stylish one-piece swimsuit.

Marilyn wearing one of Travilla's designs as Lois Laurel in *Monkey Business*. The added touches of a slight mandarin collar and both the sash and sleeves being trimmed in pom-poms give a slightly eclectic look, which matches her character in the film.

ABOVE The pom pom dress from the back.

LEFT Marilyn posing for the costume test shot for the pom pom dress.

River of No Return

"Only yesterdat she was the honky-tonk dancer, the gambler's doll, the sultry ballad singer. But today she was a woman in love following her man through the most savage wilderness in all the Americas. Through the churning death trap of devil's teeth, through thundering gorge and ambush. Following the river of no return." These are the dramatic words from the trailer for *River of No Return* (1954) in which Marilyn plays Kay Weston, a former saloon hall singer, who must face a treacherous raft journey down a river to escape Indian attack.

These costumes have come under certain criticism from some Marilyn fans over the years, saying they were gaudy and cheap-looking. However, that means that Travilla got it exactly right. Marilyn's character was an extremely poor saloon singer, her only possession of value a pair of red shoes which she carries with her throughout the movie. These costumes had to show an element of cheapness, age and continual use. Following the script and doing his homework, Travilla created these dresses perfectly for her character.

As saloon singer, Kay Weston, Marilyn donned this rather revealing outfit to sing "I'm Going to File My Claim". It is made of green velvet with flame-red chiffon layers trimmed in gold.

OPPOSITE One of the publicity shots for *River of No Return*. The Christmas colours are vibrant and perfect for Marilyn's role in this movie.

LEFT One of Marilyn's costume test shots for *River of No Return*.

Marilyn wore this dress to sing the title song "River of No Return". The gold fabric is covered in tiny gold bugle beads. Inside is yards and yards of red tulle edged in gold and sewn into layers. At the back, fabrics of pale gold velvet and a stiff lamé are pulled and pleated together to make a rough bustle, both fabrics falling into a train. The dress is trimmed in swirled patterns of red beaded tassels attached to netting then sewn onto the dress. The left shoulder has handmade silk flowers also made to look like they have seen better days.

TOP Marilyn singing "River No Return" wearing the famous yellow dress in a still from the movie.

ABOVE & BELOW RIGHT Front and back views of the yellow showgirl costume. The different types of fabric used – lamé, velvet and tulle – are all visible.

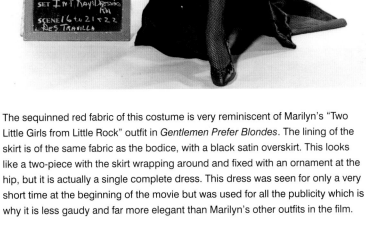

The sequinned red fabric of this costume is very reminiscent of Marilyn's "Two Little Girls from Little Rock" outfit in *Gentlemen Prefer Blondes*. The lining of the skirt is of the same fabric as the bodice, with a black satin overskirt. This looks like a two-piece with the skirt wrapping around and fixed with an ornament at the hip, but it is actually a single complete dress. This dress was seen for only a very short time at the beginning of the movie but was used for all the publicity which is why it is less gaudy and far more elegant than Marilyn's other outfits in the film.

TOP LEFT Marilyn mirrors the pose of the sketch in this test shot.

ABOVE Travilla's sketch for the costume for *River of No Return*. The dress was only seen briefly in the film.

This outfit (opposite) was worn when Marilyn is in the wilderness with Matt Calder (Robert Mitchum) and his son Mark (Tommy Rettig). She is seen washing her clothes out while wearing it and it is extremely sexy even though it reveals absolutely nothing.

Putting Marilyn in denim, leather and a cowboy hat and boots (right) does little to hide her feminine charms.

In an outfit worn only for publicity shots (below), Marilyn's corseted mid-section strongly echoes the shape of the guitar on which she is leaning. Another actress dressed by Travilla, Corrine Calvet, wore the same corset in *Powder River* (1953).

ABOVE Marilyn in a cowboy costume.

LEFT A publicity shot for *River of No Return*.

OPPOSITE Marilyn was so beautiful that she even looks good in loose fitting underwear.

How to Marry a Millionaire

This flowing purple gown was originally worn for Marilyn's dance scene with
Lauren Bacall in the penthouse apartment in *How to Marry a Millionaire*. However,
this was cut from the final production.

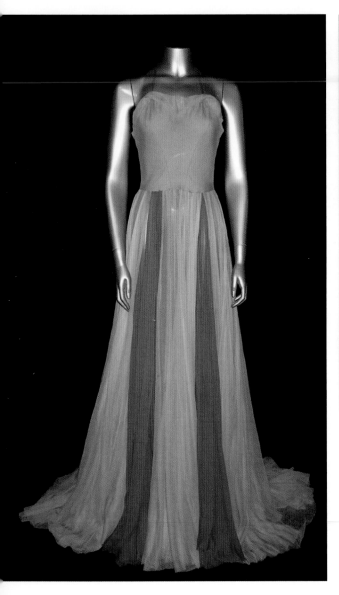

ABOVE The back view of this beautiful
flowing gown.

LEFT The stunning eautifull lavender
and purple gown created for *There's no
Business like Show Business*.

There's No Business Like Show Business

This light green dressing gown was designed by Travilla for *There's No Business Like Show Business*, although the scenes in which Marilyn wears it were cut from the final film. Both this dress and the purple dress on the preceeding page are now in the collection of Greg Schreiner.

BELOW LEFT The green crepe dress for *There's No Business Like Show Business*. It is simlar to a coat dress and has a lemon interior.

BELOW RIGHT The back view of the dress shows the amount of fabric used.

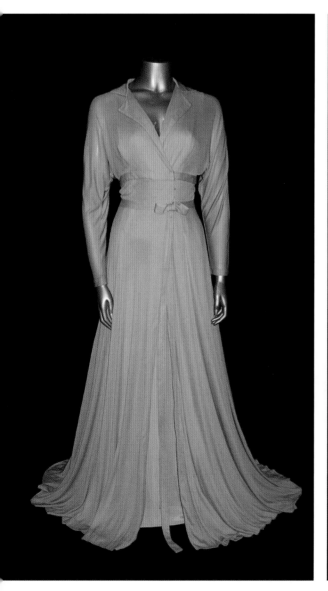

In the scene Marilyn in which Marilyn wears this suit, she makes a fuss about wearing a particular dress, saying: "Heliotrope, hydrangea, petunia, whatever you call it, it's still the wrong shade of purple". In contrast, the dress, fur and gloves for this pale grey-beige suit match almost perfectly, even though they are all made from different fabrics.

Travilla's original sketch of Marilyn in *No Busiess Like Show Business* is shown opposite. It is my personal favourite of all his sketches.

OPPOSITE Travilla's original sketch for Marilyn in *There's No Business Like Show Business*.

LEFT The dress created from the sketch.

Marilyn's "After You Get What You Want You Don't Want It" dress from *There's No Business Like Show Business* was originally designed with a split almost up to her hip. However, the exposed area was filled with pleated chiffon and the number reshot for screenings in countries where a woman's exposed leg was considered risqué. Here the dress has the added fabric.

The dress has a nude lining to make Marilyn appear as if she is naked with only the crystal areas covering her modesty. The jewelled areas are hand-sewn crystals, beads and sequins. Some areas are in the shape of leaves and others are starbursts. In some areas, thin pieces of crin spill out from behind the beading, while in others strings of beads are sewn to allow movement. Crin is made of polyester and is mostly used to support hemlines of dresses, particularly long dresses, helping the hem keep its shape so the skirt will hang better.

The headdress and jewelled area at the hip are handmade out of crin topped with sequins in the shape of flowers. The spray around the face and the hip are also made of thinly cut crin. (Courtesy of David Gainsborough Roberts).

ABOVE A close-up shot of the dress which shows the detail of the silver beads, sequins, crystals and crin that all added to its drama.

OPPOSITE A full-length shot of the showgirl dress with its feathered adornment and matching headdress.

LEFT Marilyn having her make-up applied in preparation for her famous routine in *There's No Business Like Show Business*.

PAGE 180 Marilyn performing in the dress.

PAGE 181 Travilla's original sketch for the dress.

Marilyn Monroe
"There's no business
like Showbusiness"
20th Century Fox

Travilla

As a rule, Marilyn refused to wear the full 1950s-style skirts as Cinemascope had an unfortunate effect of making the body seem wider. It is obvious why she made an exception for this floaty, feminine and gorgeously constructed dress.

The dress is made of the palest pink silk chiffon. Hand-embroidered red and pink flowers are individually sewn in layers to add depth and create almost a 3-D effect as some petals are stitched down while others are not. From the complex bodice it flows into an A-line skirt which ends at mid-calf. To add extra volume, without being structured, four panels of chiffon coming out from under the flowers were added, two at the front and two at the back. These moved in the same way as a full skirt would. A pale pink satin ribbon runs under the bust, is tied in a bow under the left breast, and then continues around to become the shoulder straps. As a final touch, a matching scarf – made of the same pale pink chiffon and also with flowers sewn on it – was added.

ABOVE Marilyn playing hairdresser.

LEFT Marilyn's costume test shot for the flowered dress she wore in *There's No Business Like Show Business*.

OPPOSITE Marilyn and Marlon Brandon standing together on the set of his film *Desiree* (1954) in which he played Napoleon Bonaparte. Marilyn must have borrowed this dress for her visit to the set.

183

This dress is visually stunning. Starting with a cream dress, Travilla encased it in sheer cream chiffon. The chiffon has tiny gold stars all over it that are actually part of the fabric. Around the ruched bodice are hundreds of hand-sewn clear crystals in different shapes and sizes which are hung from threads of crystals so they move when the wearer moves. Just below the hips the colour of the crystals changes from clear to blue. And, if this were not enough to dazzle, blue sequins are sewn all around the bottom section of the dress.

The dress is ruched up to the left hip where the main element of this dress starts. Hundreds of hand-cut tulle circles, also covered in blue sequins, are individually sewn along the split and the hem line. When looking at this dress the eyes dance over it, not quite knowing which area to focus on. (Copyright of *Colección Maite Minguez Ricart*, www.colecciónmaiteminguez.com).

ABOVE A close-up of some of the crystals on this stunning costume.

TOP A rare candid shot of Marilyn on set.

LEFT The closing scene of *There's No Business Like Show Business* in which Marilyn wore the blue dress.

OPPOSITE Travilla's sketch of the blue dress.

Marilyn Monroe
"There's no business like
Show business"
20th Century Fox

Travilla

Author's Acknowledgements

Gregory Silva: Greg is the guy who I re-connected with in the "Interview with the author" chapter of this book. Without him this whole collection would never have happened. I want to thank him for so many things. He always listened to me when I was having problems, worked incredibly hard behind the scenes and deserves his place in all of this. He alone knows the troubles and stresses that came with this collection. His constant support has been the saving grace to everything I have achieved. With love and affection always!

Giorgio Dimakis: A man who takes care of Bill Sarris, a job he takes very seriously and unselfishly however difficult and challenging it can be. He worked with Travilla for many years and independently saved the entire collection from a fire in the early nineties. We have him to thank that the collection is still with us. I have to personally thank him for his help and trust and treating me like one of the family.

Eric Woodard: A die hard Marilyn fan and a close companion to the Travilla estate, he came into my life at a difficult time and helped me see a future for the collection. He has helped me out greatly by always being in my corner, his research and constant support has been invaluable. He is always there to help me and I owe him so much.

Joshua Greene: Joshua helped me to understand the ramifications of writing a book. He helped me to understand the process and was always there to listen when I was getting hysterical. He also assists in licensing Travilla's work through his company. www.archiveimages.com

Jacqueline Capron: A true friend and confidant. Someone who has always been there for me and whom I adore. Her friendship and love has got me through some tough times, thank you Jac! Now; "Is the bar open?"

Suzie Kennedy: Someone who was there when the chips were down. She has been a tireless supporter of me and the Travilla collection from the beginning. A fabulous performer and the best Marilyn lookalike out there. She is brilliant to talk to, just never take her to a bar with videos playing.

Steve Ullathorne: A great mate and the best photographer ever. He has taken pictures of the collection, me and pretty much everything I have ever asked of him. He is always there to help. And has the most incredible eye. A true genius. Thank you Steve

Greg Schreiner: One of the leading experts on everything Marilyn. He opened his doors and friendship to me, even letting me view and photograph his incredible collection. I cannot thank him enough for his support and friendship.

Scott Fortner: The other Marilyn expert and again an incredible source of knowledge. He gave me access to some stunning photos. He listened to me ramble on many occasions, putting me back on track with all the drama that can surround Marilyn. An honest and lovely guy.

Robert Nelson and Michael Novarese: Robert thank you for your continued support and to Michael who gave me a lovely gift by telling me: "you have done justice to Travilla, you should be proud of yourself". Rest in peace Michael.

Michelle Morgan: What a lovely lady. The author of, in my opinion, the best ever book on Marilyn, *Marilyn Monroe: Private and Undisclosed*. As an author herself she saved me from imploding on many occasions. Our long "putting the world to rights talks" have been invaluable. Thank you Michelle.

Christina Blake: And everyone at PR4; the best PR team in the UK for their incredible support from the beginning and the lovely Chrissie, for our amazing friendship.

David Wills: A brilliant and acclaimed author, he has just finished writing a beautiful book called, *Marilyn Monroe: Metamorphosis*. He was totally unselfish with in his time and support for this book. Amazing. Thank you.

Kevin Freeman: Of Renaissance of Brighton. An amazing designer. Thank you for letting me interview you. You truly are a genius.

David Gainsborough Roberts: Thank you for allowing me to see and touch your incredible collection and for the amazing pictures you allowed me to use.

Kent Adamson: An author of a great book *The Life and Work of Ann Savage* who gave me so much information on Ann and Travilla's relationship. Thank you Kent. The Ann Savage Archive

Kim Goodwin: A lovely guy who shared with me some amazing pictures and also showed his incredible talent at so many things.

Dawn Jones: Has always been there for me. She helped at the shows, taught me so much and is one of the kindest people I have ever met.

Sue Bateman: Of Art House Licensing. A lovely lady who has helped so much in bringing Travilla's work to life, www.arthouselicensing.co.uk

Linda Gray: Thank you for the forword to this book. And for being a good friend and supporter of both Travilla and myself. You're beautiful inside and out.

Donna Mills: A lovely lady and someone who did me the honour of wearing vintage Travilla to an awards ceremony and looked incredible. Thank you for making time for me.

Debbie Reynolds: She is Hollywood through and through. An amazing lady and someone I have the utmost respect for. Thank you.

Debora Landis: And Natasha who have been so kind and helpful to me.

20th Century Fox and Warner Brothers: For opening their doors to me and allowing me to see things others don't.

Profiles in History: For helping me with some of the images. Thanks Joe.

Darren Julien: Of Julian's Auction House in LA for being so helpful and allowing me to use one of their images.

Travis Jaggers: Whose passing left an indelible impression on my heart. Travis if you were still here I know you would be so very proud, as I always was of you!.

Thank you to:
The immortal Marilyn Monroe and the genius that was William Travilla
www.travillatour.com

Word count up! Sorry if I did not mention you personally but thank you to all the friends and family who made this possible; you know who you are!

Filmography

1980'S FILM AND TELEVISION

My Wicked, Wicked Ways... The Legend of Errol Flynn (1985) (TV)
Dallas (1984) (TV)
A Streetcar Named Desire (1984) (TV) (costumes: Ann Margret)
"The Thorn Birds" (1983) (mini)TV)
Jacqueline Bouvier Kennedy (1981) (TV
Evita Peron (1981) (TV)
The Silent Lovers (1980) (TV) ... aka Moviola: The Silent Lovers (USA)
The Scarlett O'Hara War (1980) (TV) ... aka Moviola: The Scarlett O'Hara War (USA)
This Year's Blonde (1980) (TV) ... aka Moviola: This Year's Blonde (USA) ... aka The Secret Love of Marilyn Monroe (USA: reissue title)
Caboblanco (1980) ... aka Caboblanco... Where Legends Are Born (International, English title: long title)

1970'S FILM AND TELEVISION

She's Dressed to Kill (1979) (TV) ... aka Someone's Killing the World's Greatest Models
WUSA (1970)

1960'S FILM AND TELEVISION

Daddy's Gone A-Hunting (1969)
The Big Cube (1969) ... aka Terrón de azúcar, El (Mexico)
The Secret Life of an American Wife (1968
Valley of the Dolls (1967)
Signpost to Murder (1964) (Miss Woodward's gowns)
Take Her, She's Mine (1963)
The Stripper (1963) ... aka Woman of Summer (UK)
Mary, Mary (1963)
From the Terrace (1960)

1950'S FILM AND TELEVISION

The Fuzzy Pink Nightgown (1957)
Bus Stop (1956) ... aka The Wrong Kind of Girl
The Proud Ones (1956)
23 Paces to Baker Street (1956)
The Revolt of Mamie Stover (1956)
The Bottom of the Bottle (1956) ... aka Beyond the River (UK)
The Lieutenant Wore Skirts (1956)
The Rains of Ranchipur (1955)
Gentlemen Marry Brunettes (1955)
The Tall Men (1955)
The Left Hand of God (1955)
How to Be Very, Very Popular (1955)
The Seven Year Itch (1955)
White Feather (1955)
There's No Business Like Show Business
(1954) .. aka Irving Berlin's There's No Business Like Show Business (USA: complete title)
Black Widow (1954)
The Gambler from Natchez (1954)
The Raid (1954)
Broken Lance (1954)
Garden of Evil (1954)
Princess of the Nile (1954)
River of No Return (1954)
The Rocket Man (1954)
Hell and High Water (1954)
Three Young Texans (1954)
Man in the Attic (1953)
King of the Khyber Rifles (1953)
How to Marry a Millionaire (1953)
"Letter to Loretta" (1953) TV Series (gowns: Loretta Young) ... aka The Loretta Young Show Gentlemen Prefer Blondes (1953) ... aka Howard Hawks' Gentlemen Prefer Pickup on South Street (1953)
The Farmer Takes a Wife (1953)
Powder River (1953)
The Girl Next Door (1953)
Down Among the Sheltering Palms (1953)
Bloodhounds of Broadway (1952)
Monkey Business (1952) ... aka Howard Hawks' Monkey Business (UK)
Dreamboat (1952)
Don't Bother to Knock (1952)
She's Working Her Way Through College (1952)
Lydia Bailey (1952)
The Pride of St. Louis (1952)
Viva Zapata! (1952)
The Day the Earth Stood Still (1951)
Meet Me After the Show (1951)
Take Care of My Little Girl (1951)
Half Angel (1951) (as William Travilla)
On the Riviera (1951)
Rawhide (1951) ... aka Desperate Siege (USA: reissue title)
Bird of Paradise (1951)
Woman on the Run (1950)
American Guerrilla in the Philippines (1950) ... aka I Shall Return (UK)
I'll Get By (1950)
Mister 880 (1950)
No Way Out (1950)
The Gunfighter (1950)
Panic in the Streets (1950)
The Daughter of Rosie O'Grady (1950)
Mother Didn't Tell Me (1950)
When Willie Comes Marching Home (1950)

1940'S FILM AND TELEVISION

The Inspector General (1949)
Dancing in the Dark (1949)
Look for the Silver Lining (1949)

Flamingo Road (1949)
Good Sam (1948) (costumes: Miss Sheridan)
Two Guys from Texas (1948) ... aka Two Texas Knights (UK)
Escape Me Never (1947)
That Hagen Girl (1947)
Cry Wolf (1947)
Love and Learn (1947)
Nora Prentiss (1947)
Ever Since Venus (1944)
The Woman of the Town (1943) (gowns)
Two Señoritas from Chicago (1943)
The Desperadoes (1943) (costumes: Miss Trevor)
Redhead from Manhattan (1943)
Two Yanks in Trinidad (1942)
Fiesta (1941) ... aka Gaiety (USA: reissue title)

1930'S FILM AND TELEVISION

Travilla ghost sketched several films while working at Western Costume and Jack's of Hollywood including *Hop-a-Long Cassidy (1935)* and Tom Mix Western Serials.

Index

Page numbers in italic
type refer to pictures
or their captions.

Credits

Picture Credits

The publishers would like to thank the following sources for their kind permission to reproduce the pictures in this book.

Key: t = top, b = bottom, c = centre, l = left and r = right

Alamy Images: /Interfoto: 184
Corbis: /Bettmann: 17, 111, /Sunset Boulevard: 50, 170
Getty Images: 16, 21 t, 21 b, 22, 26, 65, 110, 114, /Michael Ochs Archive: 23, /Popperfoto: 21 c, 44
The Kobal Collection: /20th Century Fox: 19, 39, 119
Press Association Images: /AP Photo: 123
Rex Features: 121, /Everett Collection: 20

Every effort has been made to acknowledge correctly and contact the source and/or copyright holder of each picture and Carlton Books Limited apologises for any unintentional errors or omissions, which will be corrected in future editions of this book.

The following images were kindly provided by the author:
Steve Ullathorne www.@ullapix.com: 6, 68, 69, 80, 81 r, 83 r, 84, 85 l, 95, 96,139 r, 146, 147
The Estate of William Travilla – Bill Sarris/Giorgos Dimakis: 8, 9, 12, 15, 25, 27, 28, 30, 31, 32, 33, 35, 36, 37, 41, 42, 46, 47, 49, 56, 57, 58, 61, 70, 77, 78, 79, 82, 94, 99, 102, 108, 112, 113, 128, 131, 134, 137, 138, 140, 150, 156 r,161, 171, 176, 181, 185
Profiles in History www.profilesinhisotry.com: 55, 105, 115, 156 l and c,170r, 187
David Gainsborough Roberts: 54, 152, 153, 161 l, 178 r, 179
Idaho State University Library: 132, 133
Maite Minguez Ricart. www.coleccionmaiteminguez.com: 165, 184 r
Greg Schreiner and Scott Fortner www.themarilynmonrosite.com: 74, 75, 140 l, 141, 142, 174, 175
Darren at Julian's Auctions. www.juliensauctions.com: 142
Other images kindly donated by friends of the estate including Kim Goodwin

Publishers' Credits
Executive Editor: Jennifer Barr
Additional editorial work: Alice Payne, Jane Birch, Jane McIntosh, Anne Barratt, Catherine Rubinstein, Gemma Maclagan, Vanessa Daubney, Katie Arora
Design Manager: Lucy Coley
Designer: Barbara Zuniga
Production Controller: Maria Petalidou
Picture Manager: Steve Behan